DIVORCE AND THE AFTERMATH

by

SUZIE TEE

DIVORCE AND THE AFTERMATH
Copyright © SUZIE TEE 2011

First published by Zeus Publications 2011
http://www.zeus-publications.com
P.O. Box 2554
Burleigh M.D.C.
QLD 4220
Australia.

The National Library of Australia Cataloguing-in-Publication

Author: Tee, Suzie.

Title: Divorce and the aftermath.

ISBN: 978-1-921919-18-3 (pbk.)

Subjects: Tee, Suzie.
Divorced women--Biography.
Man-woman relationships.
Adultery.

Dewey Number: 306.893092

This book is a work of non-fiction.

The author asserts her moral rights.
The author takes full responsibility for the contents of this book.

© Cover Design—Zeus Publications 2011
Proudly printed in Australia

MY DEDICATION

How many times do we ignore our instincts and what our investigative mind is trying to tell us? Well, eventually we have no choice but to listen and that is what my story is about.

After 19 years of marriage, it suddenly dawned on me that it was time to face the ugly truth, so I did, after it was staring at me fair square in my face. There was no denying the truth any longer as I had done for so many years prior.

Divorce and the Aftermath is dedicated to all the men and women in the world who gave of themselves selflessly to their marital relationship, only to end up with feelings of betrayal and stripped of all their self-esteem. Whose families have been torn apart purely for lust?

My book expresses a way of getting one's self pride back, turning the pain around and showing how making life-changing decisions whilst going through such emotional turmoil, can only make it so much worse.

In telling my story and the mistakes I may have made, I hope it somehow helps those of you to understand your journey.

The positive outcomes that you and only you can bring into your life no matter what happens to you can be the turning point at any given time.

It can be a life-changing experience, allowing your life to move forward for the better.

I call it a better life, after all you must remember it's not what happens to you it's how you deal with it and I hope you can deal with it better than I did.

MY SPECIAL DEDICATION

To my mother, Elsie, who has always been a tower of strength and has taught me to believe in myself. A woman who has gone through her own battles in life and taught me that no matter what life throws at you to never give up; she is not just my mother; she was and is my best friend.

Also to my dear friend, Andrea, who has been my best friend for the last 28 years. She lived in Brisbane and even though she was so far away, there was not a day went by that she did not phone me. She was so supportive over so many awful years.

More importantly, she never judged me over the many mistakes that I may have made and I believe that to be true friendship.

Chapter 1

MY STORY

My story begins 22 years ago, a time when I chose not to listen to my instincts, as far back as when Bryce, my ex-husband and I started dating.

The telltale signs were there all those years ago but I chose not to listen to them, which was the beginning of the end for me and it took me 22 years to wake up; but I finally did. After all, some people never do.

Bryce was eight years my junior and was very arrogant with loads of confidence and a certain charm when I first met him.

He liked everyone to think he was really successful and had plenty of money but that was not how it was, in the beginning anyway.

He was and is to this day, a compulsive liar.

I fell in love with him although I knew he was very controlling and, unfortunately, I mistook that for believing a man like that was a real man, a tower of strength, how wrong I was! He was the type of person that would help anyone in a crisis, particularly married women who were going through relationship problems. I learned as time went on he just liked to play the hero. It was all for self-gratification and not for the right reasons.

My first clue was the pornography books that he continually hid in the boot of his car or in a locked briefcase, you know, the pornography that comes in a sealed plastic bag. And still after being caught red-handed, denying ownership; his excuses were very imaginative but believable.

I should have realised who he really was then but I didn't. I was in love; he was a romantic and I was in love with the thought of being in love. I should have listened to my mother, who constantly reminded me that love is blind; she was so right.

We dated for a couple of years before we were married and I have to say to this day it seems like yesterday. Now when I look back and reminisce I cannot understand why I did not recognise what was always in front of me. Bryce was the best liar I had ever met. I used to find love letters in his car when we started dating and he would tell me they were a joke from one of his friends; I believed him. It should have been another clue, where was my intelligence?

Our wedding day finally arrived, with no expense spared, but there was just something not right. I felt so ill and doubled over in so much pain, so much so that I could hardly walk down the aisle. I came to understand later that my body was trying to tell me that this was a big mistake; one that I would regret for the rest of my life. It is called listening to your instincts!

After being married for a couple of years Bryce asked me if I would have his children. I was 35 years old at the time, I already had two teenage children from a previous marriage but those three little words always got to me, "I LOVE YOU," as he would say...probably too often.

It's funny when I think back to those early days and realise the universe had given me so many clues as to whom Bryce really was, but I always ignored them. Even after being married for less than 12 months, I had found a private bank account where Bryce had saved all his commission cheques, leaving me to think he was doing poorly in his job and money was so tight. The arguments would follow but he always managed to give me hope and we would move on as we always did. This was a habit that would take me years to break.

Not long after that, I became pregnant and when the time came for me to give birth to our first son, I was aged 35 and 37 when I had our second. He was over the moon, a real doting dad. He was wonderful for the first couple of years of fatherhood and that was probably the happiest time in our married life but it wasn't to be for long.

Not long after giving birth to Bryce's second son everything started to change, life was never to be the same, not for me or our children.

Bryce started coming home late at night from work with many excuses. One of my favourites he would use frequently was that he was with a client and I always believed him.

As I said before, there were plenty of clues the universe would send me on many occasions, but looking back, I don't think I wanted to know.

After our second son was about six months of age we decided to sell and move to a new area. I thought that was just what we needed, a new start. I learned in time it truly doesn't matter how many times you move, you always take the problem with you.

We sold our first home after renovating and moved into our new home. I thought we were a happy family but I was so wrong.

It wasn't long after we moved that Bryce started to go on interstate trips with his work and the tale started to unfold. A tale that would nearly destroy everything I ever believed in.

Bryce returned home from work early one afternoon only to tell me that he was leaving. I was devastated, our youngest child was about to turn one year old and his father was not going to be around.

I asked myself continually, "How can this doting father, my husband, turn into this monster that I don't know?" I could not describe him any other way.

He did not offer any explanation at the time except that he had been seeing a psychiatrist; she had told him that he had been persecuted by me, how dramatic I thought. I knew then he was lying; he had not been seeing a psychiatrist at all – he was just manipulating me to make me feel bad.

I will never forget the word 'persecuted', what was he talking about? After all, up to that point, our lives were not that bad, I thought, what did he see that I didn't? I continued to question myself, which is what he wanted me to do, place the blame on myself when he had a plan all along. It is called manipulation; he was and is still a master at it.

Bryce's family, mother, father, brothers and girlfriends had just been down the previous weekend all the way from the country for a dinner party and everyone was so happy. From memory, they were all dancing and laughing, how could one day make a difference? I felt I was living in a bad dream, how could this be? I continued to question myself day and night.

I don't think I will ever forget that feeling when Bryce packed his bags and got into his car one cloudy afternoon and didn't even look back. His four-year-old son chased his car down the road, screaming hysterically, "Daddy, come back."

Our son was an emotional mess, it broke my heart and changed me and my little four-year-old son's life forever, leaving my child with insecurities he would feel for the rest of his life. I will always remember that date; it was my dad's birthday February 18th, 1992, we had been getting ready to go to his birthday party.

We went through so much pain; I lost weight rapidly through shock and the days got longer and longer, and the nights were worse. I drank to rid myself of the pain, took up smoking and cried every day and every night. I had no idea where Bryce had gone, he was missing for a month and then eventually he made contact. He wasn't even with us for Easter and I continually asked myself over and over how he could just disappear leaving me and our boys in so much pain.

He told me it was over, he hated me, and I couldn't quite come to terms with his insults or his change of personality.

He would visit infrequently, calling me a fucking slut as he walked through the front door but the words that followed I will never forget.

He would look me straight in the eye, saying to me repeatedly that he wished I would die; this was not the same man I had married. I could not believe what I was hearing, there had to be some reason for Bryce's change of behaviour, but of course there was! Just remember that word 'manipulation'.

Chapter 2

GOTCHA FINALLY

As the story unravelled and the truth reared its ugly head, I would understand so much more clearly. When a man or woman acts in this way it always means guilt, there is someone else waiting in the shadows. A change of behaviour is a sure signal; even their behaviour in bed is a giveaway.

After realising that this was the way it was going to be I decided I had to be strong and regain what self respect I had left. I had to move on.

I didn't know what to do about anything at the time but what I knew I needed to do was to get custody of my children to protect them. I went to a lawyer who asked me where Bryce had been before all this happened. I told him he had been at a conference with his work in Sydney and he told me without a blink of an eye, "Your husband is having an affair," I said there was no way that he would do that to me.

My initial thought was that he had suffered a nervous breakdown, although most of my friends and family said the same thing, that he was having an affair, but I continued to defend him.

In fact, I will never forget that dark, dismal and stormy Mother's Day in 1992 when his parents came to visit me, blaming me for upsetting Bryce. I can hear his mother now as she continually questioned me and kept asking what I had done to her son. She felt he could be suicidal and it was entirely my fault. When I told them what my lawyer had suspected, an affair, they were horrified and said, "Not our son, he would never do that." Later I became aware of just how naive I was; my lawyer was right.

He told me that when your partner changes so drastically, you can be sure there is always someone else in the wings, I have never forgotten that, it was a moment suspended in time.

I had to get on with it for the sake of my children. I had no choice. The penny dropped! I realised I was going to be on my own and needed to provide my babies with some stability.

After being a full time mother at home, I knew I had to go back to work so I could provide a good life for them. It was all up to me. I went to night school to enable myself to get a job in real estate and it wasn't long after that I secured a position on a part-time basis as a property manager.

Bryce had even missed his youngest son's first birthday, his first steps. That was the sort of dad he had become. I know many mums and dads would not be able to comprehend how any father or mother could miss these precious moments.

He was sharing a townhouse with an older woman about half an hour's drive from where we were living. When I questioned who this woman was, he said she was just a friend. I once again believed him. Even after all that had happened, I was still oblivious. I had no reason to suspect anything else because of her age. She was 10 years older than me and I was eight years older than Bryce so I never thought anything of it, her name was Ruth. She was 18 years his senior, a grandmother, why would I suspect they were having an affair? I learned later he had spent Easter with Ruth and her family in a place called Wollongong in New South Wales.

In fact, I remember taking our boys to visit Bryce at the townhouse he was renting with Ruth. It was plush of course, it had to be for Bryce, as he had always lived in a superficial world and made out he was something that he was not. I never suspected anything, but I never met Ruth either so there was no reason to be suspicious. I needed to take the boys to see their dad because my eldest son would scream every day and every night. He needed Bryce and missed him terribly; I had no choice. I prayed every night, with Bryce's grandmother's bible, that he would come home and, as the old saying goes, "Be careful what you wish for," but in my case, what I prayed for! If anyone can imagine it was the worst time in my life up to that point. This was a man who truly manipulated my life from start to finish; I couldn't bear my little boys to be so hurt and missing their dad so much, I just wanted my family together.

Three months had passed and I was just getting back on my feet when 'lo and behold' Bryce called me on his 30th birthday to ask if he could see me. I didn't want to go but he said it was important. I was just getting my life back on track. I had even been asked out that day on a date; that was a first for me but of course, I didn't go. It was the last thing on my mind.

I met Bryce at a local hotel, I could not understand what he wanted and he sounded so serious. Then came truth time, he blurted out that he had never meant to hurt me and that it was all a mistake. He wanted to come home. He was so apologetic and kept telling me how much he truly loved me but insisted I must know the whole truth, the truth about Ruth, his lover, the woman he had been living with. He was covering his tracks and he knew if he didn't tell me, she would, and he claimed he only had sex with her once; did he think I was an absolute fool? Well yes, I suppose I had given him enough reasons to think I would believe anything that came out of his mouth, but not this time.

Later I found out that Bryce had spent a considerable amount of our savings to move Ruth from Wollongong to Melbourne. She was the mystery woman at the conference in Sydney that my lawyer had previously spoken of, you know when a man changes there is always a woman involved; she was the woman.

Bryce said he needed to be honest, honest my arse...it was all manipulation, a way to get back into my life. Telling me how much he missed his family and didn't understand what had happened to him. I took the bait, after all he was the best liar I had ever known, always sincere and believable.

It is fair to say at that time I did not want to bring up our children by myself, it was not fair to me or to them although little did I realise the trust was gone forever.

I went through so much pain over the following years that could have been avoided had I realised that it would be so hard to rebuild our relationship under such circumstances. If you don't have trust you have nothing. We went to so many psychologists hoping there would be a quick fix but I learned later he couldn't even tell the truth at our weekly sessions. In fact, the psychologist later described him to me as a narcissistic personality. Who was this guy? Why did he lie so compulsively?

I let it go and just lived my life for my children, although if I am to be honest there were some happy times in those years, with the exception of the mind games that Bryce would occasionally play.

We decided to move again because there had been so many bad memories in the home we were living in, but this time we decided to build our dream home.

I remember one Father's Day, we were renting a cute old cottage at the time, while our new home was being built and life had been quite good. I had no reason to worry about anything. I was at peace with my life. However, the very day I was thinking all was great, Bryce received a text and, when I asked who it was, his reply was, "It was my boss wishing me a Happy Father's Day." My first initial thought was, "Are you kidding?" It was actually a woman named Claire, not his boss, who I will talk about further into this story. I thought, please God not again!

My youngest son had a football game that day; it wasn't a great day, it started with an argument and ended with an argument. Bryce went one step further this time with his manipulation.

The argument was getting heated then, unexpectedly, Bryce told the boys, who were only eight and ten years old at the time, to go into the spare room with him and lock the door. He took the phone with him taking the handle off the outside of the door so I could not get in. I could not for the life of me understand what the hell was going on and then I realised that I was banging on the door making a scene whilst he was on the phone to my eldest children, telling them I was insane. Guess what, for a short time they believed him, they could hear me yelling and banging on the door to let me in.

The boys were frightened and God only knows what was going through their heads at the time. It wasn't until years later I exposed him for the true bastard he was. This had become a volatile relationship, one that should not had ever been, one that was destined to finish.

However, we moved past that episode, I can't remember how, but we did and life went back to normal for a while.

We built our dream home, it was gorgeous, a real family home. I felt this was going to be great for our kids and I finally felt that Bryce had changed. Wrong! He had just become better with his lies and deceit, which unbeknown to me were about to further unravel.

We moved into our new home in December 2000. I remember thinking, "Wow, what a great year for new beginnings." I truly was the optimist.

We finally seemed happy. Then one sunny afternoon at the end of January 2001, Bryce was out in the garden speaking to a contractor about our driveway, and I was standing in our home office. As I was gazing out of the window, looking at him thinking all was great with the world, he received a text message. By this time I hated texts! My immediate thought was not to look, trust him, but when you have been hurt as I had been previously curiosity got the better, I had to look.

I was shocked to see a teddy bear come up on the screen. It was from a woman named Claire asking him to call her with kisses. Remember it was Claire some time ago who texted and wished Bryce a Happy Father's Day. My stomach just cramped thinking 'here we go again'. Our life had become a habit. There would be a few years of happiness and then Bryce would take me again and again on his merry-go-round.

As soon as Bryce came through the front door, I confronted him. He responded as he always had, with his lies… "Oh that…it was just a friend." Yeah right, I thought to myself.

I decided to let it go, but the following week I couldn't get the text off my mind; my instinct was telling me that there was more to this, so I planted a tape recorder behind the bookcase. I thought it was the perfect opportunity to find out the truth about Claire, after all her name had popped up over the last couple of years, she had to be significant. One thing I hated was lies!

It was the perfect opportunity for me to learn the truth as Bryce then worked from home and he had the house to himself whilst I was at work. I conveniently had one of those tape recorders that only went on when there was noise in the room.

That's when I started to play his game but, unbeknown to me, the game would consume my every thought, it became like an addiction and I had to catch him. I couldn't wait to get home and listen to the day's events.

I arrived home, "Hello Sweetheart," I would say and then I would discreetly pick up my tape from the bookshelf and go to the shops where I would sit in my car and listen for some time.

Here I was, sitting at the local supermarket in the car, with a tape recorder waiting anxiously to hear the nitty gritty. However, that was not the case for some weeks as all I heard was heavy breathing, women screaming and making odd sounds. It took me a while to work out that Bryce had been looking at a porn site on his computer, which I came to learn he did frequently with his day, so much for working!

Then one afternoon after about a month of listening to a tape a day, I came home from work at lunchtime and took the tape recorder back with me. I was working full time then for a large newspaper company. I will never forget sitting in the underground car park at work listening and waiting. Then all of a sudden, I heard voices, sprung! I didn't know whether I was excited or heartbroken. It was Claire; she had phoned him from Surfers Paradise.

Bryce answered and the conversation went like this, "Hello sweetheart, yes I miss you too. I am struggling here, we are trying for the kids' sake, I have to make it work this time and yes we will stay in touch. I am not going to lose you," Bryce said.

I still have that tape to this day, for some reason I just could never dispose of it.

What a bastard, I thought to myself, this was all news to me. I had no idea we were trying to hold it together. Who was this guy?

I was crushed once again...how many times does one have to endure her husband's infidelity? I understand what most women would be thinking right now, why would she have stuck it out so long? Allow me to explain.

I had a vision of giving my children the perfect family life having had gone through a prior marriage and bringing up children on my own. I didn't want to go through that again, so I hung on to that dream for as long as I could, even though it wasn't realistic. My children deserved to have everything I had wanted ever since I was a child...a happy home.

My initial thought was, here we go again; I had to confront him, so I did. He started with the excuses and at that point I decided to take matters into my own hands. I knew Claire had worked with Bryce in his previous job.

He travelled to Surfers on a regular basis and I remembered he had mentioned a woman named Claire he had worked with at the time and that was where this little rendezvous started. She was also married. My immediate thought was, 'why do I have to go through this pain'? If it's good enough for me, it's good enough for her. I rang her work and enquired to her surname, pretending to be a client. I then proceeded to call her husband; fortunately, they were listed in the local phone book. Her husband was a feisty Italian man who was not the type to be crossed.

I introduced myself and proceeded to fill him in on the conversation I heard between his wife and my husband. He was initially displeased but after speaking to Claire he calmed down, she had put her own spin on it. She convinced her husband I was an overprotective wife and that Bryce and her were just good friends.

He believed her, but at the same time spoke to Bryce and said if he ever found out anything different he would fly down to Melbourne on the next plane and break his legs.

Once again, it all blew over, only to rear its ugly head with a new lover in the wings. I believe for many years later Bryce still kept in contact with Claire, maybe he still does to this day.

Bryce finally landed a new job and, as I said, he was in and out of work many times over the years.

I believe now looking back, he mixed work with pleasure, which is why he always became unstuck and always lost his job.

His excuses continued and it all became so monotonous. I look back now and think, what was he trying to achieve? He must have been so unhappy in life. Why wasn't his family ever enough?

It really makes me wonder why men and women are so deceitful when they could have it all. Why does anyone have to suffer, especially the children?

The next three years were not all bad, as Bryce had been working from home again. He had created his own business and was quite successful. He was even doing some cooking, everything was starting to seem normal and the way family life should be. I thought once again that maybe finally all I had been through had been worth hanging on for the sake of our children.

After all the heartache and endurance, my dream for my family was finally coming true. Bryce was a different person when he was not working for a company travelling interstate all the time. The opportunities to meet other women were not possible being at home; the temptation had been removed.

Happy times were here at last but not for long, Bryce became bored after three years working from home. He started applying for positions that took him away from us and finally landed a National sales role. Our lives were about to change forever, none of us would ever be the same again.

Bryce had been in his new role for only a few months, he was hardly ever home. Travelling on business regularly to all states and New Zealand frequently, something was not right again. I could feel it, my instinct was starting to kick in again and I was finally ready to move on.

This time there was no denying the truth that I had been living a lie for years. I had to face myself in the mirror; I had wasted 22 years of my life thinking that I could change Bryce. Let me tell you, nobody ever really changes and I learned that the hard way.

I will never forget that morning October 16th, 2004, I was so happy. My boys were happy everything seemed right with the world.

It was a Saturday morning, Bryce rolled over gave me a kiss and said, "Good morning, Sweetheart," little did I know my family's life was about to fall apart.

He went to have a shower and I could not turn that little voice in my head off that said I needed to check his phone. I had not forgotten the day before I was in the car with him and the phone had rung. The problem was that he did not leave it on hands free to talk to the person on the other end. He obviously did not want me to hear the conversation and, when I asked who it was, he told me that it was just a client.

I jumped out of bed whilst he was in the shower and found his phone in the car. I took it back to bed with me, my heart was pounding, and there was a message.

I asked myself 'did I really want to listen'? I had no choice; I had to know the truth. Had he changed? No more excuses. My instinct was so strong I just had to listen to a message that would change our lives forever and believe me, sometimes I wish I had never heard it.

I dialled message bank 101, it was a woman named Deb saying to Bryce 'Hi lover, it's only me, give me a call when you can, love you.' I felt sick and then heard him coming out of the bathroom. I quickly dumped the phone into my bedside table drawer. What a foolish move that was!

He got dressed and then went to his car only to come back in a few seconds asking if I had seen his phone and then I really felt sick.

Little did I realise he would pick up my phone and call his to see where it was. Silly me – forgot to turn his phone off and, bingo! I was caught red handed.

I stumbled on my words…the phone was ringing in my drawer. I had no choice but to tell the truth. I said, "By the way you have a message from your lover." He gasped and said, "You have to be kidding." Bryce looked at me with that look he always gave me when he was not telling the truth. There is a lot to be said about body language, his lip always went up with a slight grin.

I had come to realise every time I saw that expression whatever came out of his mouth was a lie!

My heart was still pounding! Then he had the utter gall to say it was a friend playing a joke on him. I had heard that explanation so many times before. He obviously had come to believe I was such a fool and so gullible. I was so easy to manipulate and I suppose I had given him every reason to think that way; after all it had taken me so many years to discover he was not real and believe it.

I decided to play it cool. He even made a joke about it to our two sons, making out I was crazy, he said to them, "What a funny joke someone has played on me," and unfortunately our boys believed him and they thought I was being ridiculous. Once again he was manipulating and getting away with it. Bryce actually loved playing mind games.

Our boys were only 12 and 14 years of age by this time so one could not expect them to believe there was any truth in what they were hearing, after all they trusted and loved their dad. How could any man or woman bring their children into it to save themselves, so much for a loving dad!

I decided I would play dumb and let him believe that I trusted him. But in the meantime I would hire a private investigator and tap into his message bank in his phone to expose him once and for all. Looking back, I desperately wanted to hold our family together for the sake of our children, and I realise now I excused a lot of bad behaviour, but I was no fool. There comes a time where one has to face reality, have self respect, it was just never meant to be. When I married Bryce, I truly loved him and I did not deserve what he had put our family through. I had given up so much at my age to have his children only to end up being hurt and alone as time went on. In fact I remember telling Bryce I could never have children if I thought for one moment that I would ever be left to raise them on my own, as I had done before with my eldest children, and he promised me that would never happen.

I was in Melbourne and through my girlfriend found a great private investigator in Brisbane who said he could help me. I needed to get into his phone accounts and check the numbers he had been calling. I needed proof so my boys would not turn against me although I knew they would be devastated.

I could feel my behaviour becoming addictive; needing to learn the real truth about this man. I was desperate to expose him for who he really was to everyone that knew him; after all, he was just a coward. I was prepared to do whatever necessary to get the truth. Suddenly that was all that was important to me and I became obsessive!

John, my private investigator, went to great lengths to confiscate phone bills from the company my husband was working for at the time; quite illegal, but nonetheless he did get the information I needed.

Not only had my husband been calling a woman named Deb in New Zealand, in the very early hours of the morning, but he had also been calling Claire. You remember Claire; who he was involved with in the year 2000 and earlier from Surfers Paradise? I had kept her number just in case and all was about to be revealed by John, my private investigator.

That week, Bryce had a trip away, which was a good time to tap into his message bank. The trick was to put a new pin number in his phone and call him when he was in the air. It was perfect because I knew he wouldn't answer, that was the only time it would work.

The problem was though, when he received any calls I couldn't allow him to hear them, as I had already listened to them and I realised I would have to delete them, no matter how important they were, otherwise he would know that someone was tapping into his phone. When he landed, he would listen to his messages, had I not deleted them they would come up as saved messages, which would ultimately be telling him someone was listening to his messages. I could not take the risk of being caught.

I remember on his way back from a business trip there was an American guy who left a message saying, 'Hi Bryce, what the hell is going on, if you want my business return my call'. This guy was so angry he had left many messages but, even though I knew his call was of great importance, it was more important for me to cover my tracks so again and again I pressed delete.

Claire from Surfers rang him whilst he was on the plane and left a message to say she was vibrating in his pocket. That I couldn't resist! Bryce returned home and I just glared at him and said, "Who is vibrating in your pocket?" He just stared at me; he couldn't understand how I knew, and I left him guessing.

The time came to get in touch with my private investigator, John, who had asked me to call him at 5pm on the following Friday to give me the information I needed. I drove out to a quiet road and waited for his call. Strangely enough, without realising it I ended up at the same location my father had a very bad car accident, when I was only eight years old.

Do I make the call now? It was an unbelievable feeling I will never forget, it was gut wrenching, but you know what girls, it's about self respect, part of me did not want to know, the other did, you know what I mean although that sounds silly I suppose. I already knew I just didn't know how many women there had been. I took a few minutes and made the call. John answered and said, "I am so sorry," obviously there was bad news.

Then he proceeded to tell me that my husband had made many calls in the middle of the night to New Zealand. I realise now, but I didn't at the time, that there is a time difference which would confuse me later. Then John said we have the same problem with another number being dialled to Surfers Paradise…must have been hedging his bets!

Not only had Bryce been calling Deb in New Zealand in the very early hours of the morning, but he had also been calling Claire.

He must have thought he was irresistible and was so obviously deceitful to them as well.

I sat for some time in my car, so devastated…I couldn't even cry! What now? I drove home knowing that this was the end. It wasn't just about the calls; he had been travelling constantly and I knew he had been having affairs with these women.

I had to face this lie I had been living for the past 22 years of my life, but all I could think of was that I was going to hurt my boys and that was the most difficult decision I faced.

Nonetheless it just couldn't go on, I had been such a fool; I had wasted another 12 years from when he had left me in the first place, as far back as 1992 and even before we were married, I am sure he was cheating on me. I realise now I should never have taken him back, but I was the optimist looking for that family life I was aching for and never had.

I arrived home trying to be so composed, Bryce was sitting in our home office. I thought, now what? I approached him and told him that we needed to talk and asked him to go into the lounge. We hardly ever sat in the lounge, only when we had visitors or there was a special occasion as it was quite formal and I figured this was our last special occasion, the most appropriate place to end this farce of a marriage.

We sat across from each other, we were to go to a function that evening but I was the only one that would attend. I said to him, "I know what you have been doing." His comment to me was, "What do you mean?"

I then spelt out what I knew and, because he had no comeback, he knew he was done and it was over. It was such a short conversation, all over in a matter of minutes, it probably took longer to get married! I had no reservations about what I had done although I think the anger had taken control, there was no going back, and I felt humiliated as a person, just a joke.

My whole life was destroyed in a few minutes and I couldn't comprehend what was to come.

My children were my prime concern at the time and I had asked Bryce not tell them we were separating until the next morning.

I knew how upset they would be and I felt it far better that we told them together, it would still be painful and I just wanted them to believe it was going to be amicable rather than nasty. I know it wouldn't make it less painful but they needed to know they still had both parents who loved them.

That did not happen; he had to get in first that was Bryce, selfish to the core, I should have guessed he would do that. He put a real spin on his version of the truth to our boys just like I would have expected him to do, after all he was a brilliant manipulator.

My family the next morning was devastated to say the least, so much upheaval, the boys were crushed, and I felt they blamed me for destroying their family. Funny after nearly seven years I think they still feel the same way. Everything is always my fault or it's that just me feeling guilty?

I felt my life was over, my dream for my family was gone, and it wasn't going to be. Those 19 years of marriage had ended. What now? I had to face it like so many women and men do, just as I had done before. This time was different, and I knew it was really over.

Bryce had slept the previous night in one of my son's bedrooms and left the following morning, not to be seen for some time, just like when he had disappeared in 1992. He really was a coward and I cannot to this day understand how any parent can just not care about how their children are coping. He had become a heartless human being; he only cared for himself. That much I knew about the man to whom I had devoted so many years.

I decided I needed to know more after I learned he had purchased a plane ticket to New Zealand so I went back to the private investigator and had him followed. Yes, I had him followed, after all we all want to know who she was and what she looked like. I knew this was the only way I would find out; I had become so obsessive. I didn't like behaving like this, I should have taken the high road and not given it a second thought, but I needed to know everything for my own peace of mind.

My private investigator, John, had connections with the FBI who were based in New Zealand and obviously had no cases that weekend. They got the call from John and proceeded to the airport in Auckland, New Zealand. I had sent a photo to John of Bryce and it was passed on to the FBI.

The report goes like this...
October, 2004

File No. xxxx

Investigator: xxxxxxxx

1430	Commenced observations at Auckland International Airport.
1445	Flight xxx has landed and is processing.
1509	Subject exits the processing area wearing a white t-shirt, dark blue jeans and wheeling a large black suitcase.
1509	He is greeted by a female description as follows:

- Caucasian
- Aged in her 30's
- Approximately 5' 6"
- Short hair, possibly a natural brown colour but highlighted blonde, styled in a spiked and dishevelled manner
- Slightly overweight
- Fair skin

• Wearing pink t-shirt, dark blue ¾ length pants and low black slip-on shoes

1509   Subject and the female walk out of the terminal holding hands.

1509   They cross to the main car-park area and as they walk through the car park, the subject puts his arm around the female's waist.

1516   Subject places his suitcase into the boot of a red SS Commodore, registration number xxxxx. Both get into the vehicle with the subject driving and female in the passenger seat. Departs.

1528   Subject is using his cell phone while driving.

1548   Parks in Fort Street, Auckland city. Female departs the vehicle on foot and the subject sits and waits in the vehicle.

1550   Female returns to the vehicle and departs.

1611   Subject parks in Huron Street, Takapuna. Female

away from the vehicle on foot and into *Shaver Shop*. Subject sits in the vehicle and waits.

1614   Female returns to the vehicle and departs.

1619   Parks Hurstmere Road, Takapuna, outside *The Copper Room*. *The Copper Room* is a popular bar, one of many situated in this area of Takapuna.

1619   Both get out of the vehicle and sit at a footpath table outside the bar. They order drinks and food, the subject drinking beer and the female white wine and they consume a plate of potato wedges.

The subject and the female sit in chairs beside each other. Occasionally during the course of their meal and drinks, the two would kiss briefly and occasionally the subject would place his arm around the female's back in an affectionate manner.

1715   Subject enters the bar and uses the toilet and the female gets into the driver's seat of the Commodore.

1717   Subject exits the bar and female exits the vehicle. Both walk through the shops towards Takapuna Beach and walk along a reserve adjacent to the beach and return.

1753   Both into the red Commodore and to park with the female driving.

1758   Stops in Stratford Avenue, Milford, near the corner of Shakespeare Road. Subject gets out of the vehicle and crosses Stratford Avenue and onto Shakespeare Road. He goes out of sight to us for approximately 10 seconds then returns to the vehicle, gets into the passenger seat and they depart.

1805   Parks in the driveway of xx Hogans Road, Glenfield.

1805   Female gets out of the vehicle, clears the mailbox and both then enter the house and go out of sight.

1805

xxxx is a vehicle already parked in the driveway beside the Commodore. Three other vehicles are parked at the address but registration numbers are not visible.

1816

Commodore departs with the subject driving and female in the passenger seat.

1826

Parks at a block of shops at xxx Rosedale Road, Albany. The shops are known as Rosedale Park Village. The buildings in the complex are two levels with the downstairs level being shops and commercial premises and the upstairs levels, apartments.

1826

Subject removes his suitcase from the boot of the vehicle and both enter a doorway beside *Oriental Groceries* shop. A doorway provides access to an apartment upstairs. Upstair's windows have vertical Venetian blinds which are closed preventing any view into the apartment.

1915   Stand down.

That's all I needed to confirm what I already knew, the end to the puzzle at last. John sent me pictures of the two of them together and I have to say when I saw Deb my first reaction was one of disbelief that Bryce would want such a woman, very different, devilish for want of a better description.

Where to now? I had no idea. I was so confused and left with the two boys he wanted so desperately. Interestingly enough he really couldn't care less; what a complete bastard.

I actually phoned Deb not realising that the number I had found for her was her work number not her home. She didn't answer and I proceeded to leave her a message letting her know how disgusted I was that she had destroyed my family. She worked for Bryce in the New Zealand office and unbeknown to me her boss came to work that morning and heard the message. Bryce was horrified when he was called into the Melbourne office to be confronted by what was on the answering machine and obviously it didn't go down to well after all this was one of his employees. Again as I mentioned this is always where Bryce became unstuck having affairs with his staff.

I don't know the excuse Bryce gave his superiors that day but I am sure he was inventive because Deb was the one who ended up without a job.

He managed to hang onto his position for a while but in the end the inevitable happened and he was out of work once again.

I became so angry with this whole situation and decided I would write a letter to her husband, after all I had her address from the private investigator's report, so I thought 'why should she get away with it?' Not that I placed all the blame on her but she knew he was married and I had a low tolerance for women who went after married men.

My letter was direct and to the point and I gave him a detailed account of everything I knew that had taken place. It was a relief when I sent it without a return address so I don't know to this day what happened to her or whether she ever received my letter.

Thinking back, this behaviour was no different from when I met Bryce 22 years prior.

I had been working as a manager in a restaurant; Bryce came down one night, and played the piano because his brother worked there too, which is how we met in the first place.

I was married at the time but it was not a good marriage, we had both been unfaithful to each other, and I think realised we were so young when we married. I was just 17 years of age and my husband then had just turned 19. We had grown in different directions although he did want to try to save our marriage but I had lost any feeling I had for him, more so after meeting Bryce.

If I was to be completely honest, I fell in love with Bryce after he pursued me for so long. I allowed it to happen so I suppose this is what they call karma for me. He didn't care that I was a married woman. Bryce went after whatever he wanted and there was no stopping him. He even befriended my husband at the time which looking back now, I feel is pretty low. I had experienced Bryce first hand in that situation and never realised that was who he was. He liked the chase and he didn't care who he hurt as long as he won in the end.

I didn't feel guilty at first, because my first husband drank too much and was a womaniser. I was lonely and looking for love; after all I was only 28 years of age and Bryce was there but much younger than me. He spoiled me and made me feel so special and back then you could say I was the selfish one. I didn't put my children from my first marriage before Bryce when I should have because I was so caught up in my own feelings. Love is a very powerful feeling that makes us do things we would not normally do.

I don't know whether Bryce just liked the chase or he was really in love with me in the beginning or maybe it was that our boys were meant to be here. Who knows? It just was a relationship that should never have been.

I do have so many regrets but I am over punishing myself. We are who we are and we all make mistakes. I am very aware through my own situation that I had many lessons to learn through my own behaviour and the mistakes I chose to make, but I was a faithful person to Bryce for all those 22 years I knew him, and I had learned from my previous marriage that what I had done was so wrong. It wasn't fair that my eldest children went through so much either, but I didn't desert them as he did with ours.

Some of my friends had said to me to just turn a blind eye, he will get past this behaviour and you will still have your family but what family?

How can you have a family knowing your husband or wife is continually cheating on you? What sort of marriage is that? Didn't I deserve better? The answer is, "Yes I did!"

Lonely and devastated, no one to turn to, I was on my own with two resentful teenage boys. I still to this day do not understand any of this, or how I got to this point.

I was lonely and isolated, money was a problem and how would I keep my dream home?

In the meantime I lived day by day, drank a lot which I suppose was not the right thing to do, but it got me through every day and every night, after all so many years of my life had just been snatched from under me. I am not making excuses; that's just what happens in reality although, if I had known then what I know now, I would have been much stronger and coped far better with the situation. These days I always keep top of mind, 'what does not break us makes us stronger'.

I still followed Bryce's movements, he had disappeared for a month as he usually did, and he didn't even contact his boys.

Unfortunately during that time my father passed away a month after Bryce had left; even my father had continually asked where he was. I just let Dad think Bryce was always on a business trip, I didn't want to upset him and he died never knowing what had really happened. How much more was I supposed to go through?

I couldn't do anything for my dad as he was gone. My children became my focus, and I remember often thinking to myself how can anyone that does this call themselves a parent. Children should be the priority; after all, we bring them into this world we have an obligation to see them through to adults and make their life a good one, but it's obvious with so many divorces people in today's society just don't get it.

I had learned from my previous marriage the lessons I was meant to learn. Through my own experience, I see so much selfishness in parents now that put themselves continually before their children's needs. They think buying them things they don't need is okay, letting themselves off the hook so to speak. The end result is that the children end up with the wrong values; they think it is okay and this is our society today, so destructive.

I heard Bryce was going on an overseas trip and it just so happened I knew his password for his credit card. I could follow his every move and I did. I was far from getting over what had happened and I had to know more, his personality intrigued me.

I logged on as I did every morning and was just horrified to see he was off to America, which was the dream holiday he had planned for our family, but this was not to be. His companion was Deb from New Zealand, who was married with a child, his mistress. It was like history was repeating itself; no different from when I had met Bryce, after all at one time I was the married woman.

I hope those reading my story see the significant lessons I had to go through to get to the other side. It happens to all of us that make mistakes. The lessons are real and they do happen.

I was with them every step of their trip. I became obsessed, watching everywhere they went; they had no idea. Not that it was fun but it did become obsessive not really something I should want to know, after all we were separated.

He spent a lot of money on Deb; I was just so devastated. Why wouldn't I be? This was the trip of a lifetime, one my boys and I should have taken with him, the trip we had spoken about so often, but that was not how it was. I had to move on but could not seem to stop myself from looking several times a day; it just made everything so much worse. It was an addiction which I couldn't break.

When Bryce returned, I asked him about his trip and he denied it all, not knowing of course that I had watched his every move, what a liar, I thought! At the end of the day what sort of person, a so-called devoted husband and loving father could do what he had? It was all so surreal and unbelievable!

To this day, I still don't get any of it at all, but I wonder does anyone really know each other? After all, this happens in so many marriages. The only difference is that some try to protect their children, not in Bryce's case. It is whether you have integrity and honesty, it is whether you really have love for your children and I would like to think most of us want to protect those we love. I had learned a lot by this time about myself and the mistakes I had made.

I still struggle to this day watching my boys struggle with who their father really is and why wouldn't they feel that way? They felt abandoned, no male mentor, no mate, no dad, no real sense of family.

Life had to go on regardless, so I decided to sell the dream home and, fortunately for me, Bryce's guilt got the better of him and he decided to let me have the house, which was one good thing that came out of it. It allowed me to try to start a new life but it was so hard, the most difficult thing I have ever had to do. Remember, Bryce was just over eight years younger than I was and it was going to be harder for me to build another life.

I sold our home and moved to a rental, funny enough *this* man that had given me our home had bought a townhouse in the same street, I couldn't believe it. He obviously had his own stash of money.

Out of 70,000 properties, we ended up in the same street; mind you, he thought I had followed him, how wrong he was. How presumptuous of him! Why would I?

It was good for the boys that they could see their dad but that became a disaster as well. He did not really want to see them at all. He put up with a couple of weekends here and there and then nothing. The boys went through hell and back not understanding their father at all. They didn't say much to me at the time; they held it all in, but I knew they were having trouble dealing with the whole situation.

His life became about alcohol and women and, even though he had Deb and Claire, they didn't live in Melbourne.

I remember looking at his credit card account again to see what he had been up to and noticed he was bringing an unknown woman in from Canberra. I had her name and her flight details; it was obvious that she came from internet dating.

Even though we were not together, I had the urge to play private investigator, not because I cared but I had started to enjoy the game. I think insanity had kicked in!

My girlfriend and I decided to dress up and go to the airport to see who this woman was. Gina was one of my closest friends and she thought it would be such a laugh so she went along with it. She dressed up in a burka and I wore a long black wig and clothes that I wouldn't normally wear. We laughed so much throughout the airport, it was so unbelievable.

We arrived at the terminal just in time to meet the plane, no one startling to get off and Bryce was nowhere in sight. We had the right details and realised he had been waiting at the Hilton Hotel airport for her to arrive so she must have walked straight past us. I knew later that night when I arrived home that he was at the Hilton; it was on his credit card.

I have to say it was a good night; laughter is so good for the soul but a bit insane, after all I should not have cared but I had to know everything as I believe most of us do in this situation.

Then came Christmas and Bryce asked our eldest son to join him on Boxing Day at a hotel with Deb, the woman he had been involved with all along, although our son did not know who she was until later. When the penny dropped and he realised who she was he didn't know how to handle the situation he found himself in – after all, he was only 15 years old.

His first thought was not to upset his father even though he felt himself becoming frustrated and angry with Deb knowing she was his father's lover. He loved his father and did not want to alienate him in any way; he didn't want to lose him.

Worried and confused when he arrived home he wasn't himself. He didn't want to tell me for fear I would be upset and he was right I was upset and angry. How dare Bryce put our son in a situation that was so confronting? That just says so much about the character of the man.

It was at that point I decided I would never look at Bryce's credit card again. I didn't want to know where he was or what he was doing I had to move on for the sake of our boys.

We didn't see much of Bryce after that he was very rarely available to spend time with his children. The boys were still having problems and I knew I would be left to deal with them on my own.

Chapter 3

MOVING ON

Time moved on and I bought a home around the corner from Bryce. He had met a young woman named Jennifer on a plane; she was 33 and much younger than him. They fell in love and married two years later.

They moved to Brisbane in 2007 and married in 2009. Poor girl, I often wonder if she knew what she was in for. After all, they say a leopard never changes its spots. My boys rarely saw their dad although they stood up for him at his wedding. They just felt it was the right thing to do but it was far from the normal father and son relationship. If Bryce only knew what they really thought of him he would be horrified. I am hoping that I have instilled certain principles and values in them and they would understand when they have families of their own that they would never want to take after their own dad.

My girlfriend, Andrea from Brisbane, came to visit one weekend and in the early hours of the morning I received a message on my mobile from an old friend of the family, his name was Brad. He was more a friend of Bryce's family; he was very distressed; his ex-wife had just been killed in a car accident. I had known him for 25 years but couldn't understand why he was phoning me. We weren't that close at all.

I returned his call about 4am on Sunday when I heard the message he had left and he was understandably very upset. We talked for a while and I told him I would call later that day to see if there was anything I could do, which I did.

It's funny how we all get caught up in other people's lives but I suppose it was another journey I had to take. One I feel now should never have happened.

Brad had two children who lived with him, he had always had custody and I had the upmost respect for him as a dad and why wouldn't I? Because I had been married to someone who was far from deserving of my respect.

Brad's children, a boy 9 and a girl nearly 13, were very close. I had no need to suspect that he was someone I should never become involved with. No one in my family or friends ever liked him, not even my 80-year-old mother. They could see something I couldn't and as my story unravels, it will become clear why their dislike was justified.

I asked Brad and his children for dinner a couple of weeks later. I knew he was going through a hard time and because of my compassionate nature, it was not uncommon for me to try and help a family dealing with grief. We had a lovely evening and caught up again the following week and that is where I should have left well enough alone.

Coincidently, Brad was going to Surfers Paradise at the same time my boys and I were. We were staying at different hotels but still had arranged to catch up whilst we were there.

Before we left Surfers, Brad asked me out for dinner on our own and the kids all stayed back at my hotel, which should not have been a problem as my boys were older and able to keep an eye on the younger ones. Unfortunately, it didn't work out like that and it wasn't long after that they were fighting and we had to return to the hotel. I was angry with my boys but would come to learn later that Brad's son had a personality disorder. I should have walked away immediately, because Brad did not recognise the behavioural problems in his child and continually brushed them aside.

After coming back from the Gold Coast, I didn't really think much of it. A few days had passed and Brad rang asking me to have dinner with him at his home. I didn't read too much into it, after all we were just friends, but after that evening I realised we were heading in another direction and I suppose because of my loneliness and vulnerability didn't want to listen to my family or my instincts.

We started seeing each other on a regular basis even though nobody in my family was happy, but I didn't care, I was falling in love; it was all about that feeling.

When you have been hurt in the way I had been for so many years one would think there could never be trust again but I looked up to this man because he was a real dad. What I had always wanted for my kids. I was not seeing anything clearly at all.

I was falling into another trap of despair and grief only to be hurt far worse in a shorter relationship than I had ever felt before.

Brad asked me to spend the weekend, so the boys and I went the first time together; however it was a disaster again with all four kids. It wasn't going to work this way.

The following weekend I selfishly went by myself and left my boys to take care of themselves after all one was nearly 16 and the other nearly 18. I really thought they were old enough to start being responsible and look after themselves. I felt it was time I should start having a life but that was not to be the case.

I am sure you all have heard the old saying, when the cat's away the mice will play, well that was exactly what started happening. The underage drinking, the beginning of drugs and the parties became a weekend event as I started to go to Brad's every weekend leaving my boys in charge.

I wasn't fully aware that this was going on for some time until it was bought to my attention by a neighbour, and the boys seemed happy enough to have some space from me on weekends, so I never thought another thing about it.

Life with Brad and his children was really great to start with, until we decided to plan our first trip to Fiji with my boys. We had our own room and the kids had their room next to ours with an adjoining door.

It was Christmas time and everyone was getting along well, at least I thought that was the case. Then one afternoon my boys took Brad's children to the pool; that's where it all came undone.

Brad's youngest child, who was about 11 years old, started swearing at a little toddler. My eldest son told him to stop it but he continued with the F word and the C word.

The child was around three years old and the mothers sitting around the pool were horrified so my eldest son dragged him out of the pool back to our room. I will never forget Brad's face; he was so angry with my son. Nothing his son did was ever wrong. He was a child who put on an act as if he was the one being hurt. My boys had young nieces and a nephew and knew the difference between right and wrong. They did not understand Brad's son's behaviour at all.

My son probably shouldn't have dragged him back to the room, but he couldn't get him out of the pool any other way, and he wasn't hurting him as the child made out. It was all an act to get his father angry. If there is such a thing as a manipulating child Brad's son was certainly it. After all, he had learned from the best, his own father. I couldn't understand why the mothers around the pool didn't report him.

Everything that came out of Brad's son's mouth Brad believed, so that was the end of the holiday. Brad was never the same after that he blamed everyone except his son. I felt his son had a personality disorder or he was just a good actor.

I knew his mother had suffered with bipolar, which is a personality disorder however, looking back that was only what Brad told me, I now have come to believe that maybe Brad was the one with bipolar.

The trip ended abruptly and we returned home, leaving everyone unhappy. Not realising, I started blaming my boys for all the problems that arose which was wrong, as I wasn't seeing the real problem.

When we arrived home the next day, Brad called me and told me he couldn't see me anymore, I was devastated.

I couldn't understand why he couldn't get past what had happened and why he did not see what his son had done was so wrong.

A few weeks went by and I was miserable, but I knew I had to once again move on from this bad experience.

That was difficult for me as I had become so involved with Brad and then one afternoon he asked me to call into his home and see him, so I did.

He told me he couldn't be without me and we would make it work. Oh my God, where was my sense! It was all about that feeling! We started seeing each other again but this time it was different. I should mention that I came to realise that Brad was suffering from depression but, as I said earlier, I thought it could be bipolar. I became more involved and tried to give as much as I could to his family without question. Some people would describe my personality as a rescuer.

I did the shopping every weekend expecting Brad to repay me when I returned, but when I asked for what he owed me he would change the subject and, because of his delicate condition, I would drop the conversation. The money didn't seem important at the time I just wanted to help him get better and I knew he would repay me one day, I trusted him. I had become his saviour, his lifeline, someone he depended on. Brad always said to me that he needed to get away and he would feel better if we could take a trip, so I would make it happen. I took my saviour role seriously. He always asked me to take care of the bookings on my credit card and he would pay me back later. After many trips with Brad and his children, thousands and thousands of dollars later I never saw the money, I was not the saviour, I was the fool!

To cut a long story short, I was totally in love with this man who I thought was my soul mate but he just continually took from me and, after nearly three years, I realised that there was a problem. I had always been a giver, it was part of my nature, so I never saw a problem with it and it wasn't that he didn't have the money, he did but I think his attitude was why use his money when he could use mine!

Brad's home, although a bit run down, was by a lake and he had all the good things in life including a beautiful boat which was his pride and joy, so I had no reason to suspect he would use me. His children were given everything they asked for; he was a bit over the top with them.

I think he was trying to make up for the loss of their mother although I did not understand that either, because she was, according to Brad, an abusive mother, which is why he had full custody. I continued down this destructive path thinking that he would make it up to me.

I decided to sell from where I was living because Brad gave me the impression we should move in together. I should never have sold my home; it was a beautiful old house in one of the best streets in the city and Brad did not intend to move in with me. He just wanted me to have a good cash flow.

I didn't work that out for a while, but in the meantime, rented a lovely home overlooking the bay. I realise many of you reading this will be thinking how could anyone be so gullible? How could I allow anyone to use me like that? I never wanted for myself only wanted to help everyone else. I think that is underneath called a people pleaser personality and certainly wasn't a good way to be.

Then one day he told me how nice it would be for me to have a townhouse on the water around the corner from him and, once his children were older, he would sell his home and move in with me. Then we would use his money to travel together, at least that was the plan according to Brad.

It all sounded so exciting and that's exactly what I did! I was due to move in the New Year but before that could happen we went on another holiday together with his son. Brad's daughter was an exchange student overseas in France and my boys wouldn't think of going away with him. They could barely tolerate Brad and were no different from the way the rest of my family felt.

I should mention that earlier one of my friends found him on a dating service on the internet. He told me it was all a joke and one of his ex-girlfriends had placed him on it and I believed him. You would think I would have learned by then, particularly after what I had been through with Bryce.

We had broken up three times in the course of nearly three years. I had bought my new home and looked forward to living around the corner from him. The telltale signs of who he really was were always there. He had always been a very selfish lover in the bedroom; he was a real taker. Why didn't I ever get it? It should have been my first clue and he certainly wasn't a good lover.

I should have known; after all he was the only man I had ever been with, since I was 17 years of age, that had never given me an orgasm. Yes a very sad sexual existence for any woman! Brad was only interested in himself and what he could get out of any given situation.

It's funny when I think about it Bryce was the best lover I had ever had after everything we had been through I knew that was not the reason for his continual affairs and I did really miss that.

We went off on our holiday to Cairns. Brad always insisted I book and pay for it because he was always too busy and depressed but I always expected him to repay me. Again what a fool I was!

The holiday was our last, unbeknown to me. However, I am sure he knew that and used me one last time.

I only wish I had of seen the movie 'He's just not into you', maybe I would have got it earlier and it would have saved me a great deal of heartache and money. I think looking back unconsciously, I was buying affection; maybe I had no self-esteem. I think Bryce had taken that from me after seeing the type of women he had been with.

I don't think Brad or his son would have missed me if I wasn't at the resort with them; they spent every moment together leaving me to amuse myself. Not that I was jealous of the time he gave to his son it's just that it was not a normal man and woman relationship. There was no balance and to me his relationship with his son was just a bit over the top.

Our relationship was more brother and sister or someone just along for the ride. He did not appear to be in love with me at all.

I suppose if he had been a gorgeous looking man maybe there would have been good reason for me to feel the way I did but I never took any notice of people's looks. He was overweight and always dressed like a slob but that didn't matter to me; I was in love with him or at least I thought I was. It's all about that feeling, that's what gets you hooked.

Looking back, I think I admired the dad in him, he was always so attentive to his kids although not always doing the right thing by them which became sickening after a while, realising he was not who I thought he was.

In other words allowing and encouraging bad behaviour. There were many incidences that horrified me that I haven't spoken about in this book so maybe that was not really being a good dad in the first place. His daughter was not like her brother; she was always a remarkable young woman who I had a lot of time for.

There were many incidences that I felt Brad encouraged his son's bad behaviour. I remember on one occasion the boy started taunting one of their neighbours in a very deceptive way. She was a single mother who had two girls and really did nothing wrong. Brad's son would swear at her and her girls and he would always go home to his father with a different story, one that only grew hostility in his father.

After this had been going on for some time, the neighbour took a restraining order out on Brad's son and they ended up in court where I was prepared to be a witness for this lie as I had only seen what he wanted me to see. He was a very manipulative boy and to this day I believe he had a problem that his father was not aware of. I decided to find out more about the situation and I realised that Brad's son was making the whole thing up just to get his father's attention. I was so sorry for the woman and her girls who lived only a couple of doors from him.

Sometimes things are not what they seem, so I am very careful these days not to get involved in anyone's problems. Brad's son was a nightmare and I had no idea that he was so manipulating at the time although I knew he told lies. In the end, they had intervention orders out on each other and when I really thought about it, why would any sane parent allow their child to swear and abuse a neighbour, or anyone for that matter?

Brad had taken such advantage of me I was devastated and I felt so violated that another human being could blatantly lie and use me in the way that he had. Bryce was bad enough but he never drained me financially so this to me was so much worse. For nearly three years, I lived a complete lie and for 27 years his friendship was a lie too.

He was obviously never a friend in fact I don't think he ever knew what real friendship was. He was and is a user of people. Someone I didn't want in my life after all and was so glad to be rid of.

There were so many clues when I was with Brad that I should have noticed and now I look back it was so obvious. I think once again I was in love with being in love although I did always think of us as friends first and real friends would never think of using or hurting you in that way. It was all premeditated. He knew exactly what he was doing in a relationship with me. I should have known a few months before Brad ended it when we were talking about living together and his son turned around in front of him and said, "Suzie my dad will never live with you!" Yet another clue! He was only 11 years old at the time and Brad never said a word. He just looked away as if he did not hear what came out of the boy's mouth. When I approached him later about it he said I was paranoid and his son didn't know what he was talking about.

Like father like son; they were both manipulators and I know that sounds awful saying that about a child but Brad had taught him to be that way.

Even when we were away on holidays we all went jet skiing and Brad told his son to leave his hired vest on under his jumper and walk out with it. I was horrified to say the least, how could anyone teach his or her child to steal?

I made him take it back and from that point on, I was the bad person. They just didn't get right from wrong. That's another time I should have known that they were dysfunctional to say the least.

We arrived back from what was to be our last holiday together and went our separate ways. Brad didn't say much to me but I knew something was brewing. I was going away the following week with all my children and grandchildren. Brad and his son were to join us mid week in a holiday spot called Yarrawonga and even though all four of my children could not stand him, they had accepted he was part of my life.

I had seen him the weekend prior and he was quite cool to me, even in bed, not that I was missing anything. My instincts were telling me there was a problem what I didn't realise was that the problem would be no different than what I had experienced in my marriage. The man I fell in love with was no different to the man I married but to me he was much worse. He was false! Brad had bled me dry financially and emotionally in such a short time. He separated me from my own family and the only way I can describe it is to imagine if you were involved with a religious cult. It's called manipulation. That word comes to mind so often when I think about Bryce and Brad!

I left for my holiday and Brad said goodbye to me and said he would be up during the week so I thought maybe his change of personality would blow over but that was not to be.

Mid week came and I hadn't heard from him with the exception of me calling him to let him know I had arrived safely when I got to Yarrawonga.

I tried calling him a couple of times but there was no answer and then I received a text, yes a text! I had given this man everything for just on three years. I cleaned his house every weekend, nursed him back to health through his deep depression, did his shopping, fed his family, took him on holidays, looked after his children, drove him to his counselling sessions and I received a text to say he just wanted to be friends. I couldn't believe what a fool I had been and I was a fool, a big fool.

I feel embarrassed writing about it telling the world I am a first-class fool.

The upside – and yes, there is an upside; I have learned my lesson in life finally which is not to be so giving and if a man is not even giving in bed don't let him use you. I often wonder if we ever really know anyone, we come into this world alone and go out alone; it's what we attract into our lives that makes a difference. Life is just full of lessons and it seemed I had so many to learn.

On my return, he wouldn't even see me. I would email him and text him I just wanted and needed closure. I asked him to return the money he owed me for all the holidays and shopping but nothing came. Then one day I was talking to a friend who also lived on the water nearby and she told me that she had seen him with a woman; tall, long dark hair and with children. She had seen them quite often on his boat whilst I was away in Yarrawonga.

I learned later, I had met this woman the previous year. Her name was Sandra. Her son went to school with Brad's son and she had made visits to his home on several occasions with her three boys.

I never thought anything of it as she had a partner and I did not feel threatened by her in anyway although she was 15 years his junior.

I realised then I had been taken for another ride. I remembered thinking how very sad that some people find it so easy to hurt others. After all, how do these people live with themselves and their deceptions?

Brad was involved all along with another woman. I knew something was wrong when his personality changed. It is a sure giveaway that something or someone is going on. As I said, when

I was with Bryce, when a man changes, you can be sure that there is somebody else.

Obviously I had not learned my lessons when I was with Bryce which I have come to believe that if we don't learn them the first time we go through it all over again.

Chapter 4

ISOLATION

I was on a downhill spiral from that point. I started drinking and I was still smoking, I had taken it up again when I was with Brad. I knew I had to move near him in a few weeks and I was not up for it. I couldn't get my head around what had happened. Why I was such a fool? I for some reason couldn't get past my feelings of betrayal; financially and emotionally. What was wrong with me? Why was I never good enough? I felt worse than I did when Bryce cheated on me for all those years and I was alone again.

My family and friends were all so happy Brad was gone forever and they were over the moon. Everyone I knew was delighted to say the least. However, I could not understand why they didn't have any compassion for what I had been through. I was so miserable and lost.

Looking back, I now understand why they all felt that way. I wasted so much time pining after someone that was clearly not worthy of me. They could all see who Brad really was when I was so blinded.

I moved into my new home and, although very unhappy, I got through it. What we don't realise when we are going through matters of the heart, is that our children suffer because of our behaviour, which can be said about many on the same path.

Maybe that is why our society and teenagers are different today? I do blame a lot of it on divorce and the change in family life. There are so many more single mothers and fathers raising children on their own with no help from their spouses and that alone can bring on depression and changes in behaviour. Mental health in today's society is a serious issue that should be a priority to our government.

Those that have gone through a similar situation I am sure would agree when I say, one becomes oblivious to anyone else's problems when going through the aftermath of a relationship. It may sound selfish but not intentional. That is just how it is.

My boys had been through enough; they did not need more heartache around them. They had enough to cope with their dad living in Brisbane and living with a mother who drank a lot. I was just adding to their problems. The boys started going out a lot. I was so alone and started feeling very isolated. I had cut myself off from most of my friends when I was with Brad and that's the way he liked it, but in saying that, no one actually liked him.

My eldest children, now grown up with their own children, had never been a problem through the difficult years when I was going through the divorce with their father. Yes, they had issues, but they dealt with them, at least I thought they had until further down the track, years later. The problems I faced with the younger boys, even though they were 16 and 18 at the time when I was living around the corner from Brad, were horrendous. I really believe that it was not just about our own situation but the change in society. The easy access to drugs and alcohol was the downfall of many young people.

There were so many problems. I remember thinking, am I ever going to live through it? Loneliness and isolation were bad enough, but the behaviour I had to deal with was intolerable.

I felt guilty for moving so much over the past six years and not giving our children the stability I should have. I had no help from their father, Bryce, who was now living in Brisbane. I had to find a way back to sanity for all of us.

Drugs, drinking and parties bought on anger and depression but thankfully, they were never in trouble with the law.

Don't get me wrong, they were loving kids, but I could see the effects of what the divorce had done to them particularly because their father was not around to support them. Boys, no matter how old look to have a relationship with their dad, and I blamed Bryce for not doing that.

As I said previously, my dream when they were born was to give them a loving, stable home not put them through a divorce, broken relationships and hostility.

I will never understand how any man or woman for that matter can just forget they have children no matter how old they are.

Bryce maintained he was a great dad but really an absentee father who really was oblivious to what we were going through.

It was the hardest journey I travelled watching my boys suffer emotionally. The eldest of the boys was the worst. I do feel he carries insecurities as I mentioned earlier when he chased his father's car down the road after Bryce left the first time at only four years old and I am sure he remembers that awful emotional time in his life. I have tried to get him to see a psychologist but he feels he is okay, but he is not okay he has anger issues, and if not addressed he will carry them with him for the rest of his life.

We dealt with the issues as they arose and life seemed to be a continual struggle for me and for them.

I got lonelier and lonelier and started gambling which was another bad choice. I do not think anyone is aware of what loneliness can drive you to and the pokies were where lonely people went.

I got to know who they were and why they were at the pokies every week, the same expressionless faces would always be sitting in front of a machine. I know many people would not understand this situation and people should be in control of their feelings, rightly so, but no one has the right to judge others unless they can walk in the same shoes and feel what they are feeling. Loneliness is a state of mind and many have to work through it just as I did.

In my opinion, bringing pokies into our communities was one of the worst decisions our government has ever made. It was never in the best interest of families and communities I felt it just plays on vulnerable people. It only makes their situation much worse.

The government, whether communities realise it or not, has a lot to answer for.

In fact, many families today are so dysfunctional because of our government. Families have changed, after all I am sure many of you will remember the 50's, 60's and 70's when the family was so different. I feel we were the fortunate ones. We didn't have hotels closing at 5am, kids out of control, many more people killed because of drink driving, much more violence on our streets, children exposed to internet bad behaviour and pokies bleeding the vulnerable financially dry which led to many children suffering because of it.

I don't mean to take responsibility away from those that choose this way of life. Governments have to realise that the decisions they make for communities change the behaviour of those that are struggling with mental health; depression is a huge mental health issue.

Let's take violent video games and movies for example what are children now learning from at a young age? They are learning how to be violent and if they don't see it in their own home they see it in someone else's. Surely, there are people out there like me who think the same way. I believe I have the authority to speak out on this subject because I raised children in the 70's and again in the 90's onwards.

I have seen the huge shift first hand in our society and yes, I blame the government for playing a huge role in the demise of families.

Chapter 5

CONTINUING THE JOURNEY

I realised I was spending too much time alone and spending too much money in the pokies. I had to stop feeling sorry for myself.

I was being pathetic and it is not worth throwing your life away for any man or woman. Therefore, I sold my property and moved back to my hometown after six months. I had lost a lot of money moving through stamp duty on properties I had bought. It was time to make changes for the sake of my children and myself.

I went into real estate for six months and realised I was not going to make enough money to survive being on a retainer always having to pay the company back every time I made a sale. I needed a better income; I still had one of my boys at school waiting to go onto university and I needed to help him pay for his costs.

Bryce, their father, cut them both off financially when they turned 18 and would not help with education or anything else after that. It is a very difficult situation for a lot of single parents and young people today with no support. I realise many kids have put themselves through university but every year gets harder and harder for young people to survive with everyday living costs.

That is why we have homeless teenagers, who have no support all around the world.

Our education system is to blame for so many kids not fulfilling their dreams because some don't get into university if they don't get the required score for the end of year 12. I am of the belief that a pass should be enough and they still should have the opportunity and be accepted into one of our universities because what is the alternative for them? Nowhere!

What Bryce refused to realise had we been together he would have gladly paid for his son to finish his education but he had a new wife and I don't think she approved of him paying for anything. I have to say I think she is a good person it's just that she had been bought up at a young age to be self-sufficient and she felt all young people should be the same way. She was probably right in many ways but every family has different circumstances and opportunities do not always come along for young ones as they used to. We live in a very different world today. Bryce and his wife could afford to offer some support to the boys after all they certainly could afford it they had two homes, one in Brisbane and one in Melbourne.

My resentment was still there for Bryce, I felt for a long time he had the better life, no responsibility at all. A life where he only had to worry about himself. I call it a very selfish life, one that he would regret in the years to come, as he gets older. He will have no memories of his son's birthdays, getting their driving license or the many Christmas's he missed along with the everyday connection a dad has with his sons and their mates.

Maybe one day he may understand that his selfishness was never worth the heartache he put us through, so much damage was done.

It is six years now since that awful day when our family fell apart and it has been a real struggle for me to maintain my mental health. Nobody knows how I feel; only those that are going through or have experienced a similar situation would understand.

I know some people would say I was so weak and you don't need a man, but that is not true for many. It takes time to understand our journey and for everyone it is different. I think a lot of it comes from your upbringing and the insecurities within yourself.

I had not only had to deal with my own sanity raising two teenage boys but also with behavioural issues caused by drugs and alcohol.

I am sure there are many parents that have had to deal with similar issues and know that drugs are the worst thing that can happen to a family. Finally now my boys are getting on with their lives and realise the emotional rollercoaster they put us all through although they still have their moments.

I would not wish these feelings on my worst enemy and that is just what they are, 'feelings'. I have learned over the past six years through reading so many wonderful self help books that feelings can be changed so quickly, you just have to know how.

Turning a negative into a positive; feeling sad and then happy. It really is not necessary to go through all the pain and the struggle with the isolation and feeling of loneliness.

I realise that now and maybe our kids from a very young age should be taught about emotional and financial survival; after all as I said, it is all about emotions. We all have a choice. We need a program in our schools that may help many young people to learn about life skills. It could make the world of difference learning about coping mechanism. It may help in the prevention of young people committing suicide. I wish I had known how to cope with difficult situations when I was younger and maybe I would have handled what happened to me differently. I suppose many think it just comes naturally, maybe so but for many it is difficult and depends a lot on mental stability.

This is where I am right now.

I am trying to turn sadness into happiness, taking control of my feelings. I had decided to find a business that I could put all my energy in, something of interest to me. Something different, because I had come to believe if I am happy, everyone around me would be happy but more importantly I needed to get my life back.

I would say to myself where do I begin, how do I reinvent myself? I had no idea how to go about this I had never felt so out of control with who I was but I knew I had to otherwise I would not survive.

I must have applied for over 100 jobs and I knew firsthand how frustrating and horrible it was when you put your heart and soul in your applications only never to hear from most employers.

Nobody cares who you are and even though I had an excellent resume, it was so difficult to find employment and then one day my accountant said to me if I didn't get a job then I needed to buy a business otherwise I was going to go broke, then the penny dropped!

The search was on, the first thing I needed to do was list my interests, the things that made me happy, and so I did.

I narrowed it down to restaurant, café or hairdressing and beauty. I loved making people happy and making them feel good about themselves. So after months of agonising over where I was meant to be, I decided on hairdressing even though I was not a hairdresser. I was interested in beauty so I started searching the internet, day after day for months for the right business. I had limited finances and I knew whatever I chose I had to have the confidence to carry it through, as this was my last chance.

I thought with hairdressing and beauty I could manage the business and perhaps take some courses in make-up and beauty to extend it. All my family warned me not to go down this track; they had no confidence in my ability even though I knew my marketing skills would be invaluable to any business. I had to trust myself and not worry about what anyone said. If it was going to be, it was up to me, that was what I told myself every day.

Sometimes it is good to run business or personal ideas through your family and friends but not for everyone, it can stop you from moving forward, too many opinions can bring mistakes.

I had never had a problem making business decisions in fact is was the one area of my life that I was always confident about, after all I worked in media, marketing, business development, property management and had been a Councillor in local government for six years. I had no reason to feel I could not make it in any business but that was what happened to me because of my bad relationships, my self-confidence had been destroyed.

It reduced me to feeling bad about who I was; I had no confidence in any area of my life for the first time. I was running on empty and I wasn't interested in another relationship, that was not the answer for me. I just wanted to become free and financially independent. When I say, free at the age of 56 even though I had applied for many jobs, I wasn't sure I could actually work for anyone ever again. I needed to find a business that I could manage and have the freedom I yearned for which is why I decided on hairdressing and beauty.

Beauty had always been a huge industry all around the world, but more so now in the 21st century so, after giving it a lot of thought, I concluded this was where I needed to be. As I said previously I thought I had the marketing skills to grow a business.

No one agreed with me but I was not going to allow anything or anyone to hold me back. My biggest fear was that I would end up homeless and I had to remove that thought because I always believed what we think about we bring about. I still had my son to put through university and had no help from his father, I had to make it work, and I had to be sure.

Chapter 6

IN SEARCH OF HAPPINESS

I continued to search the internet for a good salon that was within my budget at the same time submitting appropriate job applications on a daily basis to cover all my bases. I had also bought a townhouse off the plan and expected it to be finished by this time, but it hadn't even started, so I was in a very delicate financial position but continued to look at the bigger picture. I knew I had to make the right move to secure a good future.

In the meantime, I looked at all opportunities big and small at the same time concentrating on better health. I knew that if I lost weight and gave up all my addictions, I would gain confidence and be ready to take on the world.

Months went by and I came across a great salon in a place called Malvern. The owner had been there for 17 years and the rent was low. It was a great location and I believed this to be the one because it was so established. My eldest son from my first marriage kept telling me I was wrong and he talked me out of it and said I was far better off going into a restaurant because I had so much knowledge of them. I wanted the salon because it meant

I could keep my home I was building and I could have both as the hair salon was less money. In the end I suppose I didn't trust myself and believed in what he was telling me after all my background was critiquing restaurants and writing editorial for them. It had been 28 years since I had actually managed a restaurant but at the same time knew it was the happiest time of my life.

My eldest son, who had been a psychiatric nurse for 14 years, wanted a change of career and aspired to becoming a chef, much to my surprise. I know now this was the real reason he talked me around. He wanted to come into the restaurant with me and live his dream although now looking back I am not sure now that was his dream. I think he watched too many master chef shows and he realised that later, it wasn't as easy as it looked.

We came across a restaurant that was more expensive than I had planned on buying but he kept on encouraging me to take the risk. My mum and I drove down to the restaurant and decided I was right it wasn't a good location. Again my son made me feel like most men did by this time that I could not make good decisions so I gave in and bought it.

Jack, my son, was so excited and I didn't want to let him down, and several times I felt like pulling out of the deal, but he continually gave me confidence to succeed and kept moving forward. I should once again have listened to my instincts! He kept telling me how proud he was of me making the right decision and I felt I had let him down when I left his father so I was making a decision based on emotional thoughts.

My daughter and youngest son kept telling me it was a mistake and would end up ruining our family. How right they were!

It is really hard being a mum when you are trying to please everyone but I had to move forward and without Jack I don't believe I would have had the courage to do that.

In saying that, I was not in a good emotional place to make such a big decision.

It was funny that he used to be the negative one; it was almost as if we had changed places. I used to be the positive one but after my failures in relationships, I had lost all confidence in making the right choices but with Jack's help, we were starting to move forward and regain the confidence I once had.

My younger boys were still a problem and still angry with the world, one in particular but I had no control over them so I had to learn to let go. I thought by being away from them for long periods whilst I worked would encourage them to grow up. My youngest was 19 years old and was starting to put his life together but the other was still struggling to find himself at 21.

Having a second family and being alone had nearly destroyed me and I knew it had to change. My eldest two children had never really been a problem; they were living on their own at 18 and were more self-sufficient. This says a lot about our society; after all they all had the same mother and all were touched by divorce although I still felt I had done something wrong to cause them to feel the way they did. If I am to be entirely honest, my mistake was giving them so much, thinking I was making it up to them for not having a dad, so yes I am to blame for that.

I hoped the restaurant would bring my family closer together and bring me the financial independence and freedom I had dreamt of. I was always a believer in the books I had read, 'The Secret' and 'The Law of Attraction', although I had not lived by their teachings in fact just the opposite which is why maybe everything seemed to go wrong up to that point in my life.

To be successful, one needs to have a positive outlook and not fear the worst. I knew that I had to change and so I told myself everyday that my life was changing for the better. I used to say to myself, if it is to be it's up to me.

The restaurant was going to be my saviour, my sanity and my freedom. At this point, I was not interested in having another relationship all I wanted was financial freedom, to prove to myself I could do it and was prepared to work harder than I had ever done before.

The restaurant was across the road from the beach on the beautiful peninsula. It was a café during the day and restaurant by night with a touch of class. I had been involved over the years in marketing and had managed a restaurant 28 years prior so I was hoping it would be like riding a bike and it would all come back to me and it did. Making the decision to buy the business nearly drove me crazy. I was for it one minute and backing off the next, it was not an easy decision to make.

I realise now when you feel that way you should not make decisions because that is your instinct telling you that you are making a mistake. I had very little confidence in myself and I understand why after looking back.

How I allowed men to treat me had made me into a person I didn't even recognise but once I signed on the dotted line it was full steam ahead.

Jack, my son, started his apprenticeship and was so excited after all here was a man nearly 39 years of age starting a new career, which I thought was rather courageous, but he loved to cook and he was able to fulfil his dream.

We finally took over and I just knew that finally I had made a good decision, I thought! One that would enhance my life, get me out of being a recluse and give me financial freedom. It wasn't just about money; it was knowing I could still help my children when they needed and once I got the business to where I wanted it to be it would give me the freedom to travel. It's really important when we get to mature age that we know it's our time and sometimes it is not possible to experience the joys of life that we wish for but always remember we have to make it happen.

I knew it would be a life change and it was the hours and the stress of having more responsibility than I had ever had in my life with the exception of raising children twice on my own.

My life was finally moving forward to a stage where there was always light at the end of the tunnel. I had rid myself of my addictions although I still had the occasional drink but never had another cigarette or gambled ever again, which was a challenge, but I did it.

As I have said previously, don't ever criticize anyone for having addictions no matter what their addiction may be because we are all guilty of having something addictive in our life and we can only encourage and try to help those that want to break free from their own addiction.

Chapter 7

WHAT I HAVE LEARNED?

Where do I begin? There have been so many lessons. Some I had to learn over and over again, particularly when it came to the type of man I was attracting and the neediness I had to overcome.

My lessons were actually just about me, how to believe in myself and be courageous making life changing decisions, to take a leap of faith. Not to judge others and certainly not to wear my heart on my sleeve for the world to see.

I always thought I needed a man to make me happy and I didn't realise happiness was within; although I still think it's wonderful if you are one of the lucky ones who have found your life partner because I never believed we were meant to go through life on our own.

My life should have been different and it would have been had I not lived with so many insecurities as a child but my parents knew no better like so many families in those days. They did the best they could. Again what we learn from our parents, many of us carry through our lives. It is simply the bad behaviour of our parents through generations, instead of learning by their mistakes and having the insight to change the patterns of life, because that's exactly what they are.

I feel my journey has been so infected by the side effects of growing up in an alcoholic family and instead of changing the pattern continued down the same destructive path. I blamed everyone and everything around me for my bad choices so I always had an excuse.

When I look back now I was a fearful child, a scared child and all I ever wanted was to feel safe and secure in a happy home where there were no conflicts.

Even growing up I was a teenage alcoholic but didn't realise it. A binge drinker is an alcoholic and I was just a child at 13 years of age.

I think being married at 17 and having a baby did not help; in fact I believe it was the beginning of the end.

My first marriage had its ups and downs, but I did not realise how important it was to me until it was over, but isn't that the way it always is? Another lesson is never to take anything for granted and the grass is never greener on the other side. I love that saying because it is so true and I am sure many of you would agree with that from your own experiences.

Alcohol plays a huge destructive part in many people's lives and they don't even realise it.

It affects the way we think, our emotions and so importantly our decision making. It is great if you can go through life and have no regrets, I have so many I would not know where to start.

Many of my lessons came from making the wrong choices; not just because of alcohol but also attracting the wrong partners in my life. I never knew how to listen to my instincts but now I am finally learning.

The biggest lesson I have learned is to stop depending on anyone else to make my life right. I have to do it myself. I realised I had to complete this journey with my children in the best possible way. To be a great role model and to show them that if I can make a success of my life, then they could as well.

I suppose this is mainly for my younger boys, not so much my eldest son and daughter from my first marriage. I was proud of them up to that time. They would have their own lessons to learn in life and I had hoped they had actually learned from my mistakes. However today's youth, a different generation, had not just alcohol but drugs to deal with everywhere they go, so my work was really cut out for me. I just had to make them realise they could have a better life than what they experienced with me.

I am not saying I was a bad mother because I was not. I did the best I could under my circumstances.

I now have the opportunity for myself and that's what the next half of my life is about, to work hard, earn my own living, be responsible for my own happiness, respect who I am and believe that my kids are proud of me and who I have become.

Chapter 8

MY BIGGEST LESSON

A couple of months in the restaurant had gone by and it was a struggle. I had bought in a seasonal location, not realising that it was like a ghost town in the winter.

I had received all the financial information before I bought the restaurant and I thought I had followed all the right procedures when purchasing a business. My accountant had looked at the figures that the owner had provided; a legal document as proof of financials.

I was so oblivious to the fact that the previous owner had lied and not just about the figures he had provided. He had made the chef part of the contract and all the staff said they would stay on. Unfortunately for me, I learned later he had told his staff that I was going to sack them all. He had several other businesses that he needed them to work in and moved them around to the different locations for his catering business on a weekly basis.

I was left with a shell, no chef and no staff.

I had to start again, here I was in another crippling situation, I couldn't believe it, I was devastated once again. I had put everything I had into the restaurant even the money I had saved for my home.

I had to be really strong and make the restaurant work otherwise I was going to end up with nothing, once again I felt ripped off, why was this happening to me? I knew why, it was because I didn't trust my own decisions and listened to my son, Jack.

The money was running out quickly even though I had hired a new chef and new floor staff we were not doing much business because it was winter and I kept telling myself I had to make it to the spring and summer, which is when the business would become viable because it was a seasonal restaurant.

In the midst of all of this, my son decided he did not want to be a chef, which once again devastated me. After all, he was a big part of the reason I bought the business. I remember having cold feet many times but he always encouraged me. I am not blaming him entirely, as this was my decision and I had to face the consequences.

Chapter 9

FAMILY DISASTER

My son went back to his job as a psychiatric nurse, fortunately for him he could do that, but I thought he would still help me out. His wife was reconciling the books and some other office work for me but it wasn't long after that I realised they both virtually walked away from me and left me to go through this enormous strain on my own.

The arguments in the family started and I saw a side to my eldest children from my first marriage I had not seen before, a selfish side.

Here I was struggling to survive on my own and the only people who supported me were my nieces.

They were two beautiful girls who offered to work for me for nothing. Not only were they beautiful they were amazing young women who have taught me the real meaning of family. They had lost their father to cancer some years previously and said to me when you lose someone you love it makes you more compassionate and considerate to any family situation.

Families become more precious!

My family was broken in a way I had not experienced before. My eldest son and his wife had deserted me and that hurt more than anything. It's true what they say, never go into a business with family? I should have listened to that and I felt so cheated.

I was not giving up; things were getting to a point where I felt like I was living just day to day. I had to get through it and all I could think about was getting to spring hoping for better weather when people would actually want to go out. It had been the worst winter for 15 years that we had known and I had to stay strong with no sign of relief in sight.

I had decided to put the restaurant back on the market. I was doing most shifts by myself with the exception of Friday and Saturday nights trying to keep the costs down. I was even laundering the napkins, tea towels, all the cleaning of the restaurant. I had to save on costs. I had no choice and my body was feeling the effects, sometimes I could hardly walk.

I just prayed every day that the restaurant would sell and the days and nights grew longer and longer. "If only", I would say to myself on a daily basis if only I had not been so naive, why couldn't I make the right choices why and how did I end up in this mess? Why did I buy a business in a town that was a holiday destination? It was so isolated and the locals did not support their restaurants. My eldest sister had also warned me she hated this small town for her own reasons.

I couldn't dwell on it; I felt like I was going crazy and money was running out fast, my family was dysfunctional and I only had myself to blame after all it was my decision regardless of any encouragement I received from my son. I just kept praying that I would sell the restaurant and come out on top. This whole experience had taught me the value of money and the importance of keeping a job. These last six years of my life had been a nightmare, one I just wanted to move on from and start again. If I just kept the money I got after the sale of our family home, I would have been fine and could have lived off the interest.

I really would not have needed to work had I done it right. In hindsight that sounds great, but in reality who knows?

I wanted to completely wipe the slate clean and start making good choices for my life, find a good job. I also knew at my age that was going to be difficult keeping in mind I had put in for over 100 jobs in the last year before I had bought the business, which was another reason that I looked for a business in the first place.

Spring was fast approaching and I was not feeling well every bone in my body ached. The chef was right; it was a young person's business; not for someone who was nearly 60 years of age. With the stress of it all, I took up smoking again.

Alone and horrified of what was to become of me, I kept going and spring was fast approaching. At the same time, I was trying to keep a positive approach. My mother had always been a strong force in my mind not to give up. She was an amazing woman who didn't depend on anyone, she always had so much faith and I knew I had to be more like her.

It's not that I didn't believe in who I was at that time; I just felt broken and started questioning why this was happening to me and what was the lesson this time I was supposed to be learning? I tried always to do the right thing by others, but sometimes that was no benefit, as wrong as that may sound. I felt as if I was being punished and for what?

It had come down to the crunch; it was only two weeks to September school holidays and I was down to nothing financially. I knew the weekend would either make or break me and on top of that, three of my best staff were off, it couldn't get any worse.

I had to stay strong and my body was telling me to give up. I had never felt those aches and the pains before, not like this, my weary hands and legs had to make it.

I still was battling with the betrayal of my son and his wife, which was really getting to me, however, I knew nothing was going to change if I didn't. I just had to get on with it on my own and stay focused. I remember a couple of nights, when we would pick up on the weekends, my niece telling me to call my son and his wife and ask them to come into help, but they wouldn't even do that even though they knew I was desperate.

It was always my belief that families were there through thick and thin to support each other in times of need but not in my case. I was angry all the time but at the same time knew that what I was feeling was not going to get me anywhere, I was alone and that was how it was, I had to accept it. There was no white knight in shining amour to help me nor was there going to be.

I still questioned though why my past relationships that infected my life to begin with were doing so well, Bryce and Brad, after all they seemed to have it all. I couldn't understand why I was the one who had to go through what I called hell.

They had their relationships and their homes yet they were to me the evil ones who were partially responsible for where I was in my life. I suppose I sound like the victim and even though I felt I was I had to get my mind off that and start concentrating on being the winner in all this if I was to survive.

There were times in my life I just felt like throwing in the towel. I didn't want to be here anymore but then something would kick in and I would tell myself that I would win in the end.

It is true what they say when you keep looking back it stops you from moving forward. I had to start getting rid of the past and stop being the victim.

Life had not been kind, but in saying that, I had many opportunities that could have worked but I was always looking for something else. I was never satisfied with what I had when I had it but isn't that what we are taught? To look at the bigger picture and go for it. I had never been a risk taker and I looked at others who had made it but I suppose we don't see what goes on under the surface, it always looked so easy.

I had been stripped of my confidence ever since I had given up the job I loved at the newspaper to become a Councillor in local government, a poor paying position to try and help my community, a thankless, tireless job that was not worth all the heartache and pain.

It was obvious by now I had always chosen the wrong path for my life; I had to start making the right choices and get my confidence back to do that, but how?

Chapter 10

WHO AM I?

I started to wonder who I really was. I was a woman, a mother, an employer, so many depended on me. I had to start gaining the confidence for my business to survive and I knew that much about me. I was and am a survivor. My responsibility was to myself first, and then to others. I think that's where I went wrong I had always put others first instead of looking after me. I was known as the rescuer.

Now it was time to take the bull by the horns and get to where I wanted to be, and that was a successful woman in my own right, after all I had been too busy looking after everyone to think about myself.

It was spring, the better weather was coming and I had every reason to believe my business would get better. There were a few interested buyers but no one had put an offer in and I kept thinking is this another lesson I have to learn? Do I have to get through this to get to the other side? Was that what the universe was trying to tell me? Hard work, don't look back and just keep going that is how I would achieve my goal.

I had bills piling up and I had to make the money last. I was living on an oily rag and I knew suppliers would start pounding on the door at any moment. It is an awful feeling to owe people money but I had to keep the business afloat and I always depended on the weekends to bring at least the wages in so I could pay those that worked for me.

The rent was overdue again and I knew the landlord would be paying me a visit, I would say to myself just stretch it out. It was always due on the 1st of the month; I tried to buy an extra couple of weeks as I knew September would be a better month with the school holidays just two weeks away.

Little by little, I would have to make it work, so I started giving suppliers just a little every week. Someone would have to wait, just how long I could go on like this was beyond me.

Weekends you would think would get better, as I said that was my bread and butter but the first week in September was not looking good, not even many for Father's Day. I didn't understand.

I had come to realise it was not the community who was going to push me forward and out of the red to the black, it was the holidaymakers and there were not many of those coming down.

I remember I kept saying when is it all going to change, everything was becoming such a strain and I just had to keep going with my mum saying to me on a daily basis don't worry just keep going, it will change. She had so much faith but it was so hard I felt my health was getting worse. Smoking again was having a bad effect on me but I didn't care at the time. I was so lonely and so confused I just felt like throwing in the towel.

I know it sounds like I felt sorry for myself and the truth is I did. My family was dysfunctional and I was so lonely and tired with no one to help me out of the mess I found myself in. None of my children would come and lend a hand.

The nights and the days just dragged on and the loneliness was unbearable. I couldn't even cry; I had no energy, I just kept feeling the despair to the point as I said I didn't want to be here anymore. I even found myself thinking how nice it would be just to go to sleep and never wake up again. I knew that was wrong but I was in such an emotional state at the time.

I used to ask myself repeatedly, why? I had done all the right things, marketing, had great food and a nice restaurant with a lovely atmosphere it really was nothing I was doing wrong. It really came down to where I was, the location. I could scream now looking back that I was so stupid getting myself into that situation in the first place. I knew I had a real problem making the right choices for my life and I just needed to turn it around but, quite frankly, I felt it was in the lap of the gods. Had I bought in spring and not winter it all would have worked out perfectly but I didn't. The money I would make in the summer would get me through the next winter and that's what everyone did who had a business in a holiday destination. I had done it all back to front and, as an elderly gentleman told me, he had seen so many restaurants close because there was no support from the locals, they just didn't go out.

My children were constantly on my mind although I knew my youngest boys were always there for me and truly loved me. The eldest of my younger two boys was living in Brisbane to try and get closer to his dad; this was the boy that ran after his dad's car when he was only four, when Bryce left him the first time. He was still insecure and just wanted a relationship with Bryce, which was never to be. He thought he could live with Bryce but that was not to be. He had to share a home with his wife's younger sister and that was not what he wanted. As I said, he wanted to rebuild his life with his father and thought he would be welcome to stay in his home even if it was just until he got on his feet. The youngest was always so busy with school and his football at the time but still both boys always called to see if I was okay. Even on Father's Day they both texted me to say Happy Father's Day. They said I deserved that because I was not only their mother but their dad as well.

My eldest son and daughter were oblivious to my feelings and didn't have the same compassion that my younger boys had. It's funny that they were all from the same family, different dads but so totally different. I just had to accept that the eldest really didn't care for me anymore. By this time, my daughter had sided with my eldest son and she didn't have much time for me at all. They were selfish, only worried about themselves; they didn't take after me they were very much like their father, whereas the younger ones had more compassion, even though they didn't come and help me in the restaurant. They had that compassion for others that is a quality that is so important in life and didn't judge me for the mistakes I had made.

It is true that we are all born with our own personality, although at the end of the day I still believed loving families should support each other through thick and thin.

I had been in the townhouse I lived in for over 12 months and my eldest daughter and eldest son had not even given me the time of day, not even a phone call just to say hi and to see if I was still living. It was apparent that no one cared which just made me feel worse and a failure as a parent.

Sorry there I go again, woe is me, playing the victim. I really had to move on and get out of this terrible state of mind I was in. I had to start looking at the positives, for the things I needed to be grateful.

I don't know where I would have been without my girlfriend Andrea who lived in Brisbane. She called me every day of every year always being supportive along with my mum and I realised if I didn't have them God knows where I would be in this lonely shell I had found myself in, so at least I wasn't alone. From time to time I had found myself thinking about all the lonely people there must be in the world that no one gives a thought about.

I thought a lot about the elderly to over that time and how a lot of families desert them when they are placed in homes and remembered when I was about 10 years old visiting them in the homes for the elderly. I would make them fans out of icy poles sticks and remembered how happy they were just having someone to talk with. I was with the Red Cross then at such a young age and it always made me happy that I was making others feel good which is where I started always being the giver. That's who I became right through my life.

I am not saying it is wrong to give I am saying that giving too much of yourself can be a mistake because so many can end up taking you for granted.

Although I knew I had to push myself to become more positive about my situation it was hard but I was determined that I had to change the way I was thinking. I had to block all the bad out and start living like the book 'The Secret', tells us to. For those who don't know 'The Secret', it is a self help book written by Rhonda Byrne. The book is very enlightening and is about the way we can attract a better life. I decided every morning I would get out of bed and look at life differently and at night visualise what I wanted when I went to bed. I wanted so much for someone to buy the restaurant and move on before it killed me.

Chapter 11

STAYING POSITIVE

How does anyone stay positive in bad situations like this? I suppose I had no choice, otherwise the inevitable would happen. I had to discipline my mind because it is all about our thoughts. Remember, what we think about we bring about.

It is not an easy task staying positive when you are looking at your bank account and you know time and money is running out but you have to. The broker had made an appointment with me on a Monday to show some people through the restaurant and they were locals so I felt that was a positive sign, as they would know the area so well. They knew that spring was the right time to buy and the restaurant was going to be so busy over the summer months, which, as I said, would set them up and carry them through the next winter. I could not survive; I didn't have enough money to get to the summer and my health was getting worse, I had to sell.

It was 5.30pm my appointment time and I was so nervous they had to be the buyers. I remember I kept saying "let this nightmare be over", it must be my turn to have a break and life can be normal again. I deserve to win this time, I deserve to have a better life and I certainly deserve to be happy.

I would visualise the restaurant selling and a sold sign right across the front window.

The appointment went well and there was another buyer interested so I knew it was going to sell. I had called the previous owner to see if he wanted to buy it back, much cheaper than I had paid him for it, but he didn't however he passed on my details to someone he thought may be interested. He was a complete bastard but never the less he did get the wheels in motion, so to speak.

In the meantime, I took some chill out time, a lunch with my favourite friends talking about the past few years and the behind closed doors stuff one does not talk about. I had not mentioned earlier in the book but there were moments I did certain things I was not proud of, but at the same time did not regret, purely because I was lonely.

I reminisced with my girlfriends about my one-night stand in Sydney, it was one of those times Brad had dropped me. I never would have thought I would have done what I did but guess what I did and for some reason it was not only good but it was right for me. I can't tell you who he was because I don't remember his name. It was too long ago but he was as I remember good looking and intelligent, too much to hope for in today's world I suppose.

I got lucky. He was a nice person as I remember, we met in a bar, I was very lonely and I think he was too. I had never ever done that before and never ever contemplated I ever would but I did and I have no regrets. I will never forget that evening with him, he was a gentleman and made me feel like a woman should. He was only 40 and a good lover exactly what the doctor ordered. I never saw him again just one night, one I would remember forever.

I wasn't going to bash myself up over it after all what happens in our private life should not be anyone else's business and I don't think anyone should sit in judgment…do you?

After all, life had not been kind to me and it was nice to spend an evening with a stranger.

The guy who knew the previous owner called to enquire about the restaurant. He already owned a restaurant in the next town and was very successful and now wanted to buy another business. I hadn't heard from the first buyers so I accepted his offer although it was $25,000 under the asking price and at that stage I didn't care, I just wanted out. The landlord was being an absolute horror to me and hassling me about the previous tenant who had not fixed certain items when he left it to me. I was not about to take on that responsibility. It was all getting so hard for this sale to go through as I had just found out I didn't have the lease transferred to me when I had bought.

What a nightmare I had found myself in. I ended up telling the landlord if he didn't let this sale go through, then we would both lose, so it was in his best interest to let me out of the lease.

I couldn't wait, although I was scared of what I was going to do to make money. Not knowing what the future would hold for me, but I kept on moving forward. All I knew was that I wanted to be out of the town I had come to hate.

It was a miserable place, although beautiful landscape and it truly was a huge mistake on my part.

I just kept thinking, "just another man who has ripped me off", and it's true these last six years I allowed so many men to completely rip me off one way or another. I had let them all get away with it and not only that, I had lived through the worst 26 weeks of my life. In saying that I had learned so much that I knew would be invaluable to me in the future.

My family was a complete disappointment; not one of my children were there to help me and that alone was enough to wonder what happened to the meaning of family?

As I said when the chips were down you should be able to depend on those closest to you but not in my case, just another lesson. A lesson I will take to my grave. I had given so much to my family my whole life. My main purpose revolved around making sure my children had everything they needed and yet here I was alone and in trouble. There was no one I could depend on.

The rent was still overdue and I had so many bills I was just hoping that the buyer would sign any day and I could start moving forward, but I still had no word from him. I was so worried.

I can't remember another time in my life I felt so helpless and I knew I had to just keep focused and couldn't allow it to get the better of me.

I felt I had really tried to be such a good person in life. It was so unfair that this was happening to me.

In the meantime I would lay in bed putting in for jobs till it was time to go to work and it was so frustrating. Someone, somewhere had to give me a break; I had to keep faith that it was all going to work out and, with the exception of my family, it would all come together. I had grown up with a lot of faith and I felt this was a real test. I had to stay strong.

I didn't feel like a failure I knew I had tried and that's all that mattered although my eldest son felt differently. He had sent me the worst email I have ever received telling me I was a fake and he knew I couldn't do anything, which I read to mean he thought I was a huge failure. He thought so little of me. That was depressing in itself and I will never forget that.

At last the contracts were signed and I had a settlement date 27th of October, 2010 and I was so relieved. I still had bills piling up so I faxed all the suppliers telling them the restaurant was sold and they would be paid on the 28th of October, which would buy me some time. It was important that I walked away clean and owed no one anything.

It was incredible timing when my chef gave a week's notice on the 6th of October and I signed the contract on the 7th. I knew I had no choice but to close on the 10$^{th;}$ what else could I do; I had no chef and my contract stated I had to stay open until the 17th.

I rang the buyer and asked him if I could leave a week earlier as I had given him permission to move in on the 18th although, as I said settlement was to be on the 27^{th,} and he agreed as he was renovating. I had to close that deal giving him $1000 worth of stock. He was an astute businessman who really didn't care about my situation. He called it 'loss of goodwill'; a bit ridiculous really when you think about it and a way of getting a bit more out of me after all as I mentioned he was closing anyway to renovate so what was another week to him?

A selfish man who couldn't care about anyone but himself. I couldn't understand how anyone could be so cold.

The last day felt such a relief. I really didn't have many staff by this stage and we all left on a lovely note. I didn't feel any regret in fact I felt so grateful that I was out of it as I had learned so many lessons in such a short time. The value of money, family and about who I was.

The business had a bad effect on my health and now I had to concentrate on my future and rebuild my life for the final time.

Chapter 12

MY NEW LIFE

I had put in so many applications for positions but no one ever replied, which once again felt like it did the previous year but this time it was different. I had lost over $128,000 in just 26 weeks and now had to find a job to rebuild my life and save for my home.

I didn't really want to go back to real estate but I saw a job advertised and the principal's name was John. I saw his picture and realised I had worked with him in 1992 when Bryce had left me the first time when my boys were only four and one year old.

He had worked for me back then as a property manager and when he left, he went into sales and bought his own business in another suburb.

He was a lovely family Italian guy and I knew this could be the way to rebuild my life and get myself into a better financial position.

The office was within 15 minutes of my home where Brad lived, he was the man I went out with who ripped me off financially and emotionally. He left me for another woman 15 years his junior. I didn't want to go back there but I couldn't let that stand in my way; I had to start a new life. John hired me on the spot and I was starting on the 20th of October, seven days before my settlement. It wasn't my dream job. I would have much preferred to have secured a position in local government as an employee, but it was not on the cards for me so maybe this was where I would get myself back on track and make some money to start again.

I have to tell you it was so scary to be in the position I found myself in. Going into a job I was not fond of but knowing at the same time if I did it right it could set me up for the rest of my life.

I knew I would make it because as I said, I am a survivor and I knew that nothing would stand in my way this time.

I had a friend who was 101 years old, that's right 101. She was a beautiful woman; her name was Doreen and an inspiration to me. It's funny that you don't know a whole lot about someone's life until the day of their funeral. She was amazing; her husband walked out on her when she was a young woman with two small boys and she worked three jobs to survive, her story really inspired me. To this day I carry her picture in my work diary to remind me that anything is possible. I hope that she knows how important she was to me, an inspiration!

Just imagine in those days being in that position and although we had never spoken about her past I knew she was an amazing woman. She gave me so much courage and she probably never even knew. It was funny because her son had told me before she passed away she had said she wanted to go into real estate with me. She didn't know at that time that it was a plan of mine to do that so maybe she knew something I didn't. Doreen celebrated her 101st birthday in my restaurant and I was so honoured to have her there. I will never forget her; she was and is my mentor, someone I aspired to be.

I had a run in with Bryce about our eldest son because he had disowned him and I will never understand how a parent can do that. Bryce left him running after his car in 1992 saying "Daddy come back", when he was only just four years old so it was no surprise to me that he was still sending the same painful message to our son. I felt sorry for my son, after all he was 21 now and his father thought so little of him. He had no direction in life, no future in anything. It had all started because our son had been living in Brisbane for three months wanting so bad to get close to his dad but realised his dad wasn't the man he thought he was. He grew lonelier and lonelier in Brisbane and decided he needed to come home. He had no family there. Bryce was always too busy with his new wife and his own life. Bryce had even sent our son a text message saying he should think of him as dead now. How could any parent say that to their child? One should never ever give up on their children and that is my belief. There is hope for everyone.

I often wonder if the world would be so different if all the parents took responsibility for those they bring into the world. Bryce had to realise that no one is perfect. We all make mistakes and that was no different for his son. Maybe time spent with him would have made the world of difference. I remember after Bryce left in 1992 our son was so traumatised my eldest sister's husband, his uncle, spent time with him and it was so comforting to this little boy who felt so deserted. They walked on the beach and had fun and to this day, he has never forgotten how special those moments were with his Godfather.

Chapter 13

OCTOBER 16TH – MEMORIES

My son was back home and I was relieved in a way as he was sitting for his police exam on the 6th anniversary since his father had walked out unbeknown to him. I prayed and prayed that morning he would pass, he just had to. He needed so much to create a future for his life and he was low on confidence by this stage. He had a car accident the day before and things were not going right. I thought, it had been six years and surely things should be changing for the better; after all, we had suffered enough and yet Bryce was living a lovely life.

How could that be? All I ever wanted was for my boys to be really happy and have a great life. After all, isn't that what most parents want for their children?

I remember thinking back to that Saturday morning when our lives changed forever. I thought I had actually moved forward but I still had resentment in me.

I just wanted so badly for both my sons to be okay and have their careers; one in the police force and one a teacher then I think I would be able to get on with my own life. At this point I realised I had been raising children for 39 years and still had not had my own life. I think most of you would agree there is something wrong with that picture and I had not really enjoyed my life up to now. I had to be the breadwinner, the mum, the dad and make all things right even though the boys were old enough to stand on their own two feet but as a parent, I felt I had not taught them to be accountable for their own lives.

I had to change the memory of this day. My son sitting his exam and me looking at yet another rental but this time in a beautiful place called Sandhurst. However, after investigating the rental market, I realised it was not going to work for me, as the rental market was so high.

The boys and I needed a change and we had to make a new beginning after the restaurant mess. This time I had to make everything work for all of us. My son would not find out for two weeks whether he passed his exam so in the meantime I had to keep moving forward even though it was the 16th and full of bad memories.

It had to be a new beginning.

I couldn't help but remember our beautiful home we had built and how I wished I was still there. It would have made such a difference if Bryce and I could have raised our boys together. Their lives would not be in such turmoil and they would not have gone through all the upheavals I put them through.

I felt so guilty and unstable as a parent although I still believed I had done the best I could for them. I did have some lovely homes and I should have realised when I had bought my first home after Bryce left that it would have been the best decision to stay there and now I would not be putting us all through the upheaval again.

In hindsight should have, could have. There I go again looking back all the time. I had to stop this behaviour and start looking only forward. I had to wake up every morning with a new dream, one that would make us all happy.

I did feel my life was moving forward finally and even though the debts were piling up I knew I would come out okay after all that is what having faith is all about. I was about to start my new job and I kept telling myself I would be successful.

Through my whole experience in the restaurant I had learned so many lessons and I was about to embark on a new journey that I would make my life.

The new owner of the restaurant was making it difficult for me by making me spend more money because of some maintenance issues he felt were my responsibility and they weren't. After all he had already taken an extra $6000 off me. Then the landlord's lawyer put his own price on just surrendering my lease and I thought, what more did I have to go through to put this mess behind me? How much did I have to lose to move forward? The fees from the landlord's lawyer were ridiculous to say the least but I had no option I had to pay whatever they asked. It was thousands.

I had to accept all the conditions they were putting on me as I was in a vulnerable position. It was costing me a fortune and there was nothing I could do but pay them. I felt just another man was ripping me off; it had become the story of my life. There was no question the landlord's lawyer had me over a barrel.

It was so unfair, but what could I do, my financial position was in their hands if I was to get out of it with something. I had to comply with the health department and fix everything even though none of this had been done by the previous tenant. I was on the home run, just two weeks to go and it would all be over.

Could it get any worse; at this stage I wasn't sure? It was all such a nightmare. My eldest son, who wanted to be the chef and disowned me, had sent me awful text messages; the "F" word used frequently saying he hated me and wanted nothing to do with me. He obviously was having financial problems, which he would not accept was his own doing, after all no one forced his wife to leave her job to go into the restaurant. It was her decision it was not my responsibility. We are all accountable for our own decisions in life. He had put no money into the restaurant so I couldn't understand why he was blaming me.

I just wanted life to move on to a better place. I knew I had lost my eldest son and his family forever; they accepted no blame in the whole restaurant fiasco. If only we could have all acknowledged our part in it we would have been fine. I loved all of my children warts and all that was a given but they didn't see the problems they caused for me. I felt sorry that my grandchildren had to go through the entire trauma. I just wanted everyone to be happy and my family to be that perfect picture.

I sat and wondered *why oh why this had to happen?*

Why can't things change? Yes I suppose I was feeling sorry for myself but understandably so at this stage.

The same old saying always came to mind "If it's going to be, it's up to me".

Now the time had come for me to go back into real estate; I had to make it work and I had to never look back but be grateful for the opportunity, after all I thought nothing could be as hard as the restaurant was.

When I took the job with John I didn't realise he only had two listings however, it was a nice office to work in and we all got along so well. I would go out walking dropping pamphlets every morning in the hope that we would get some response. John was a lovely man and very genuine. He was going through his own issues with marriage breakup and he was not in a good financial position although he was growing his property management which kept his business afloat but that was not going to help me. I realised one day at the front desk I could nearly see Brad's house from where I was sitting at reception and I was so worried about running into him, which I avoided at all costs. I couldn't help but wonder why I ended up back near Brad. It was just full of bad memories for me but was a lovely place and everyone was friendly.

Even though I had found a position in real estate, I was still in an awful mindset with my eldest children not talking to me and the only thing on my mind was setting a good example for my two youngest boys. I just had to give them some family after all they also were cut from their eldest brother's life and none of it was fair or their doing.

Luke was and is a beautiful person who I was proud of. He was my youngest and reminded me so much of my daughter; so self sufficient. They were switched on and looked for opportunity, not like the first child, Jack, who thought the world owed him something.

My life now was in turmoil waiting for the closure of the restaurant and ending up with very little money. I felt I was so over it and just wanted it all to end. I really didn't want to be here anymore and in the back of my mind were my two ex-husbands saying I would end up alone and here I was.

Where to now? I asked myself every day. Why couldn't I get a job that I really wanted and have that feeling every morning to jump out of bed and be excited about my day? I didn't think it was a lot to ask. I remember feeling like that when I was at the newspaper and I wanted that feeling so bad again.

I felt so isolated and I had no one except for my mum who had been so supportive through everything. By this time an 82-year-old woman who had taught me to be so courageous and had such high principles.

My daughter had sent me an email saying I had only myself to blame and I made my life what it is. I suppose that was true. I had made many mistakes but I was the only one who had to live with the consequences and try and change it. We all make mistakes and I never believed in putting others down because of their choices whether they were right or wrong. I wasn't a fabulous grandparent, which my eldest children resented me for, and constantly reminded me of it but I still loved my grandchildren regardless of what they thought.

I was a parent at 17 years of age and for 39 years had been raising kids and if that is seen as selfish to anyone then so be it. I never felt that way after all I had not experienced my own life up to that point even Bryce was off the hook. He was only a father for 14 years so I really felt I was a little entitled to think of myself and my own life at 57 years of age.

As I mentioned earlier, what gives anyone the right to criticize others until they walk in the same shoes and know how it feels? Our lives are all so different and each and every person handles emotions differently as I did. I felt I was starting to go through depression. No real family and a job I didn't really want but was grateful on the other hand to have something. I just had to keep pushing myself but my loneliness was getting the better of me.

I had paid out all the suppliers of the restaurant around $28,000, which was depressing to say the least, but I think worse than that was coming home to an empty house every night and staring at the four walls.

As I said I was really lonely and had no one at this point in my life.

Going to work turned out not to be that bad after all. I had an opportunity that I knew I had to make happen if I were ever to get past the way I was feeling. It didn't help still being a mother and hoping one day my youngest boys would find their lives.

This last week had been the worst for me and if it had not have been for my boys I wouldn't be here. I knew they needed me however I felt. I had to stay focused and strong.

My mum was great but she is just one person; I needed my children but they were far from supportive in my time of need.

My eldest son and his wife were never coming back into my life; I knew that. My eldest son had become someone I didn't know anymore and his wife was not the person I thought she was. She was bitter and twisted.

Life was not being fair through my eyes. I just had to keep going and I knew if I worked hard and just stayed focused, I could make it. I just had to get used to the lonely life after hours.

I will never understand unsupportive families; love is supposed to be unconditional and as I said nobody should ever be put down for making mistakes.

Chapter 14

THE PENNY DROPPED – THE MIND SHIFT

Going to work was hard enough to a job I thought I hated and then one morning after speaking to my girlfriend Andrea I was starting to realise that there was some connection between my continuous moves with jobs and homes. I had moved 31 times in my life since I was just 17 years of age. There was something wrong with that. I had been so restless since Bryce had gone six years prior and I had lost so much financially and personally, so I started to evaluate what that could mean.

I realised I had been so restless, no matter where I lived or who I worked for, that nothing would be right in my life if I didn't change. I had to become stable, stick to something and start enjoying my life. Be more confident with where I was right now in my life. It wasn't about the job or where I lived it was all about me and my confusion with life itself and everything I had been through. Quite frankly it's a wonder I have survived the last six years of turmoil.

It was time to change, get rid of my addictions and mean it. Wake up happy every day and look forward to going to work that was at least a start. Remember, misery brings more misery and I was over that feeling well and truly by now. I could be whoever I wanted to be and there was nothing that was going to stop me.

My boss, John, had said to me if I worked hard there was no reason why I couldn't buy another home within the next two years. I held onto those words because I desperately wanted my own home again and to be financially independent. I knew I could do it I just had to apply myself and make it happen.

I had been given another opportunity and this time it had to be different.

I started reading 'The Law of Attraction', again and made a promise to myself that I would only attract good things into my life.

My picture perfect family was never to be a reality and I had to accept it after all, what choice did I have?

Today would be a new beginning – one of hope for the future and no regrets. If I have learned anything through my journey, it is to never give up on yourself and just fill your mind with only positive thoughts. Shut all the people out around you that make you feel bad and surround yourself with optimistic people who enjoy your company.

I am now starting to see where my future will be and I just know my boys will be okay. They have their own journey and I am sure now I have turned the corner they will be far better off for it.

One thing we all realise in life is that it is not what happens to us but it is how we handle it and how to bring about positive change.

I made a promise to myself to look at everything in life differently and to rise above anything or anyone that gets in my way. I love the way I feel today it is a feeling of such optimism and just knowing life can be whatever I choose and not because of what happens to me. It has taken me six years to get to this point but I am finally here and that is all that matters. Success is not that far away all I had to do is reach out and touch it, make it happen.

I still wanted to move to another home; I was tired of living in a townhouse and I knew that it would be much better for me and the boys. I realised I had left my home on the water because of Brad but it wasn't that I didn't like it. It was because he was living so close to me, but I was not afraid of that feeling anymore and I was entitled to live wherever I chose.

Since working with John, I had gotten to know some of the people in the community and it was starting to feel like home.

Life with the boys though was becoming increasingly difficult particularly the eldest of the two. I am sure he always thought someone owed him a living instead of getting up and making it happen for himself. I find it hard to refuse giving him money when he needs it but I know I have to stop. There is no other way to make him understand that we are all accountable however I am fully aware I made this burden for my own back giving him so much over the years. I swear he thinks I am a money tree that will never run out.

He is not aware that it is running out and we all have to pull our weight, if we are to survive financially. I am confident I will get back on my feet, but he needs to learn about money and I find it frightening that he doesn't understand at the age of nearly 22.

Both boys had the same upbringing and yet they both handled it differently.

Young men need to understand the importance of responsibility at a young age and I don't blame him entirely. I blame myself because I am the parent, mother and father. I obviously didn't get it right. These are the times I start to feel so resentful towards Bryce, because he is also responsible after all and this is his son I am talking about. He is free and having a wonderful life with his wife and obviously carries no guilt about our boys. That to me was and is so wrong and as a parent, I could not be so irresponsible. I mean after all what was the point in having children? Why have them and say you want them only to end up leaving them? What if I had chosen to turn my back on them? What would have become of them? I shudder to think.

My life had been a rollercoaster over the past six years and now it was time to get it together and be happy. I am still having a hard time with my family. They are so dysfunctional with no end in sight. I still to this day cannot see my eldest son and his family ever coming back to me but that is out of my control. I can't do anything about that and quite frankly I am over it. They have treated me badly. I should have said to them if they wanted to be part of this family then they needed to get over it. I believe that families should be able to say what they think and move on. Not act like children and have that childish hatred that is so unbecoming in anyone. It's called maturity and sometimes it takes some of our children much longer to grow up but then it can be all too late.

Life is still a lonely place but somehow I get the feeling every now and again that it will change. I think the last emails from my eldest son closed the door forever; they were so hurtful and so unnecessary. How much should any mother endure? He wrote for the last time and the jealousy he felt for his brothers was so unbelievably sad.

"You really are warped, maybe all the alcohol has soaked up the remaining cells you have left... we bought the boys gifts you ignorant bitch every year, but whatever, and as for money why don't you get that son of yours to pay up on all the handouts he got, and as for my grandmother she can have you all as the last few times I have spoken to her all I coped was abuse about you and how I have done this, well you can all get fucked I never want to see any of your clan again...I don't blame my father or Bryce for their actions and now have no issues with Bryce as I can only imagine what it must have been like living with you. You only have to look at your life and look at your loneliness to realise who you truly are, ask yourself and be honest for the first time in your life, you are full of faults but claim to be the victim in every case and constantly burn people...your one true friend is in Queensland! Wow, do the math...distance relationships work for you as no one can stand being around you. As far as I am concerned I have divorced myself from you and want no further contact from any of you can't make it any clearer. STAY AWAY ALL

OF YOU !!!!!!!!!!!!! I can live with that and am comfortable with the same. *Your ex-son."*

And then there was this email on the same day! As I said, how much should a mother endure after all the sacrifices one makes for her children?

"My God you are truly delusional, the boys, the boys, the boys, that's all we hear, well fuck them, they are only half brothers at best who never bother with anyone but their own needs, isn't it funny how my life has to revolve around them every event, every birthday, every Christmas and if I didn't bother, well the wrath I would receive wasn't worth it...you, on occasions, do have a good heart yet that comes with conditions...you have taken from me more than you have ever possibly given...remember my wedding when I had no choice but to have Bryce as my best man because as you say, family will always be there...remember my graduation when I wasn't allowed to spend time with my father...oh my God I could go on but can't be assed...fuck the lot of you hope to never see you all ever again, you can have your perfect sons. *See ya.* "

Can anyone believe that a son could be so hostile and cruel? I have to live everyday knowing I gave up my whole life just to have him at the age of 17 and now ask myself, why? I had to put all of this out of my mind, his family no longer existed.

Every day that passed was going to get better and I was committed to making my dreams come true, that's all that mattered at the time. I was not going to let my eldest son's hostility get in my way.

The next afternoon he dumped all my paperwork from the restaurant on my back veranda. It was all kept at his home because his wife was keeping the books and even though we didn't speak, I kept her employed, so we would email for business purposes. He not only dropped paperwork, but dumped rubbish such as large flags and other items that were so unnecessary and no use to me. After his awful emails and dumping all that rubbish I decided enough was enough and he would be out of my thoughts forever.

I had to let go of this insanity once and for all.

I was feeling quite happy at work by this stage and had settled in but I had gone to see a financial advisor at the bank after I paid back to the bank the extra money I had borrowed for the restaurant. My savings were getting lower and I knew I had to change something to survive. She was great to talk to, but said to me that I needed to have a job that paid me a better wage than I had.

She explained to me if I didn't sell enough property with the real estate company I worked for on a regular basis I would run out of money very quickly. I really wasn't making enough to cover my weekly expenses so this time I had to really think long and hard about what I was going to do. On one hand, I thought that in real estate others did well why shouldn't I? But that had not been happening for me and I had not even one listing although it had only been three weeks. I had to be patient to reap the rewards; after all, Rome wasn't built in a day.

Every now and again Bryce and Brad both would creep into my mind. I felt so resentful towards them although the money situation was my own responsibility. What I had learned was that I made so many financial mistakes through my emotional state over the past six years it was my entire fault. There was no one else to blame. I should have been in control although it is not uncommon for anyone to make mistakes when making decisions whilst under so much stress.

It happens to so many people.

If I had of gone to a financial advisor years prior, I would not have found myself in this position in fact I would have lived comfortably. After all at my age I should have been looking at living a comfortable life not the other way around and at this stage in my life I couldn't help but have regrets. How on earth was I going to pull myself out of it?

I started thinking I needed to get healthy, stop smoking and lose weight that was the beginning to getting my life back. We all know how great it feels when we shed those unwanted kilos and start to look at ourselves differently. A lovely young girl named Kristee who I worked with in the office decided we were both going to tackle this problem together. We both wanted to lose weight so we made a promise that we would encourage each other to achieve our goals. I felt so good even after a couple of days. I knew I was on the right track and I just started looking at

food as the enemy after all I was still a young woman myself ev
at the age of 57. I knew in my heart there was more happins
that was to come for me if I became disciplined in everythi I
did, at least that was my dream. I knew it was all achievablend
after everything I had been through I knew more than anythg I
deserved to be happy.

Chapter15

THEY ARE JUST FEELINGS

I was walking out of my office, and low and behold there was Brad in the café next door to me. I was horrified at first, but was looking at the back of him and it suddenly dawned on me. What did I ever see in him? He was such a slob. Brad still looked the same, in the familiar baggy old shorts and his stomach protruding out over his t-shirt with nothing on his feet. I must have been insane to go out with him after all he didn't even care about his appearance.

I was so frightened of running into him but it was the best thing that could have happened to me because it made me realise those feelings I had been carrying with me. The hurt and the pain were just that 'feelings', they didn't exist. I really didn't feel any emotion at all for him and just kept walking as if I had not noticed. He was someone I wished I had never been involved with in the first place. It is good to confront one's emotions because they really are just a memory but we hang on to them for so long without realising, instead of letting them go and we realise there is a happier life out there without that person in it.

I have come to the realisation whilst writing *Divorce and the Aftermath* that I had been very driven by feelings and emotions which is something most of us don't realise. Whether we are in a relationship for three months or three years, we take those emotions and feelings with us into the next relationship, which is where it all goes wrong. Since I have stopped smoking and drinking, it feels like a dark cloud has lifted from my head and all of a sudden I can see what has happened to me and everyone around me. It truly is an amazing experience to be able to recognise how all this is possible.

You realise that a crazy moment seemed to last forever but I think to it is actually about not wanting to be alone. It's more about being insecure with yourself and once you can feel comfortable with who you are then it all starts to unravel.

The realisation is that we are all alone one way or another. I spend so much time by myself it doesn't seem to bother me at times, maybe a little some nights, but most of the time I have become accustomed to that feeling of isolation. I am not saying I wouldn't like to meet someone because I would. All I am saying is that it doesn't hurt anymore once you get used to your own company after all you have no choice sometimes that's just the way life is.

I do however sway back and forwards in my thoughts sometimes, it is unbearable but then I have to remind myself I am okay.

I am so looking forward to moving house and hoping it is soon because the place I am living in is depressing in itself. I need a change and I need it now to go onto the next chapter of my life.

Working in real estate has been difficult so say the least trying to get new listings was hard particularly since I had found out the other local agents were putting us down to potential clients. I had to figure a way around it because one way or the other I had made up my mind I was going to be a success.

I put in an application for a property in Sandhurst, which is where I believed it would be best for the boys, and I. Originally I thought it was a little expensive but I had to pay a little more than I thought because I just couldn't get anything else. Even if I had to get a second job on my only day off, I thought it would be worth it. Now, I had to be patient, something I really was not good at, waiting was always hard for me because I always seemed to be waiting for something great to come into my life. My mother was so right when she said patience is a virtue!

I got my first listing within a month of working for John and had two others on the go. I told myself everyday it was a sign of all good things to come. My boys seemed to be going backwards, in particular the eldest. He had come back from Brisbane; he had been drinking and I couldn't cope with the way things were, it had to change.

I felt the loneliness creeping into my life again it was something I had never gotten used to. I was not one of those people who could go and sit in a bar or go to a nightclub on my own, it just wasn't me. I knew time passes and I had been doing so well with not smoking and drinking I was feeling so much better losing weight as well. I wanted the old me to return; the one I loved that could look in the mirror and be full of confidence. I was a believer that life had something great in store for me. It had to and I just had to keep faith.

I don't know what it is about young people today they don't seem to have that inner strength that makes them strive for the best in life. I suppose there are some that have it but the majority I see don't. They think life owes them something and I had to find a way to change that in my boys but I had no idea how.

I thought the first step was to make them pay something towards our living expenses because they continued to think I would look after them forever.

It's funny but my youngest son said to me that his dad didn't have much money so he couldn't go to him although Bryce had two homes and a great life living the executive couple with no kids. I don't know what he thought I had when I didn't even have my own home or why he saw me as a money tree when he knew my circumstances. It didn't make any sense to me with the way either of them thought. They watched me work six days a week and couldn't even make their beds or help with the housework. I felt so bad because it had to be my fault; after all I was the one that raised them.

They should have been taught how to cook and be self-sufficient otherwise how could they live with anyone in the future? My immediate thoughts were of the poor girls they would end up with; they will just take over from where I left off. I can't help but feel responsible the way they have turned out. Don't get me wrong, they were compassionate human beings but very lazy like most teenagers I suppose.

I had been so tied up in my emotions over the last crucial six years of their life I should have been present and mindful of what I should have taught them. I had to stop bashing myself up over the 'what ifs' and it had to be now or never; although I knew the most important things I had taught them had sunk in...love and compassion.

I didn't get the property to rent in Sandhurst there were four applicants and one offered more rent than everyone else which I thought was not right but it obviously wasn't meant to be so I continued looking for the right property. My boys did not want to leave the only town they knew. It was the only home they had known. It was convenient for them. Their friends were there and they had already moved so many times they didn't want to move again.

My youngest was waiting to hear from university and he really deserved to get in but there again there was that word 'patience', it was so difficult waiting all the time for anything good to happen. He had just finished his diploma after two years and he had worked hard in that time, I was proud of him.

He wanted to be a PE teacher and had dreams of becoming an AFL coach although he didn't come out and say it I knew what direction he was heading. He had already coached an under 12's footy team for a local club for a season and now was moving onto coach another football team although this time it was under 15's.

I was proud of him because he was up against men in their 30's and he believed this was the way to climb the ladder to get to where he was going. I have no doubt in my mind he would make it because he had the ambition and drive that made him shine. He was given a team that was at the bottom of the ladder the previous year and it was up to him to bring them to the top. This was all volunteer work and he believed that this was the way to build his reputation; one that he believed would make him reach his goals.

It's sad when I think Bryce knows nothing about his son's; he wouldn't even know what their favourite colour is or anything else about their lives. Parents should be part of a child's life forever, which makes me understand a lot about their past behaviours.

The eldest of the two boys never got into the police force and decided he wanted to become a builder. He was waiting for an interview with a school to see if he could get in. I was so worried about him as he had done so many courses and I hoped this would be his chosen career. He may have been a late starter but sometimes it takes time to know the direction one needs to take.

I had no idea why he had been so lost and very different to his brother. I hoped this time he would find what he loved. He had his real estate license and only lasted for a few months working for an agent but it wasn't for him and I thought at least he had been studying. He was so much like me he had no patience to give anything he tried time to work, to see the end results. He was my biggest worry as he continued down the path of immaturity and no self worth I could only hope and pray that he would find his feet.

Life had to move on for all of us. I had made up my mind that I was going to be a high achiever and set a great example for my boys. They were just so important to me and it was going to be up to me. I had to get out and drop pamphlets more frequently on a daily basis and come up with some good promotional ideas.

I had to walk the talk, look the part and stand out from the rest of the boys. I was so excited because I felt like I was coming out of this deep dark depression that had been hanging over me like a dark cloud the past six years.

I went to an awards dinner and the top achiever was a young man who grossed $300,000 commission for the year. I had to talk to him and find out how he got to that point, how long it took him? How much patience did I need to make it happen? I could feel the excitement of all the possibilities, after all I loved where I worked and that was a start as it had been so long since I had that feeling of enjoyment in the workplace but that was only the beginning. The rest was up to me.

I couldn't believe I saw Brad again although it is a small town so I was bound to run into him from time to time. I had been in a prospective vendor's home and didn't realise that she was across the lake from his home. As I walked out to the backyard with the vendor I could see his home and then I saw him looking back at me, although I am not sure he realised it was me. I felt a flood of emotions come over me, after all they were just emotions, but this time it was not only seeing him but seeing his home and where we used to sit and his boat and remembering the fun we used to have.

I had to remind myself this was a man whom I trusted my life with, and had known for 27 years as a good friend. I felt bad that night but realised again it was just those old emotions triggering me to go back to that state of depression and I wouldn't allow myself to go there again, I was stronger than that.

I would be happy no matter what because I was a survivor. I had to believe that I would soon be very successful if I really worked hard. I kept saying to myself I don't need a man for my survival I am who I am and I will be okay emotionally and financially. It truly is a mindset and always remember what we think about we bring about. I have seen enough evidence of that to know that is true.

Chapter 16

STRIVING FOR SUCCESS

Success is not all about money. Success is in every part of our lives and I wanted to achieve all of it in every area of my life, to become financially independent. I wanted to become the perfect mother and make up for all my mistakes I thought I had made. I wanted to have that picture perfect family that I had wanted ever since I was a little girl. I hungered for it.

Even though I knew I had accomplished so much in my life. It was just bits and pieces of my life, like a puzzle. There was no stability or continuity. Looking back, I felt I had sabotaged everything good that had tried to come into my life and now I had to make sure I made the right choices as I moved forward.

A new day, the beginning of the week and I had made my mind up that I would achieve like no other.

I had two appointments to secure another two listings with John and I was so excited to get to work. I set goals that I would work towards on a daily basis and to work harder than I had ever worked in my life although nothing as I said could be harder than the restaurant was.

I had sent Bryce an email just to let him know our youngest son had finished his two-year diploma in case he was interested. I thought it was the right thing to do because I still encouraged some sort of a relationship even though it always fell on deaf ears. One day I know Bryce will regret not knowing his boys and the funny thing about this is he thinks he has a relationship with them already but nothing could be farther from the truth.

Christmas was fast approaching and I needed to make it a special year because we had the worst Christmas the previous year. Time passes so quickly and so much had happened in the last 12 months, it was all so surreal. Even though I thought life had been cruel to me, I still had so much for which to be grateful. After all, I could have been homeless because of the restaurant fiasco. I just hoped I would find another property to live in before Christmas as I dreaded being where we were. It was a depressing place to be.

The week was nearly over and I had hoped to pick up a new listing for the week but I didn't and I was feeling a bit flat. People are so strange, I had spent hours with one depressed woman who I really felt sorry for and she gave me every indication that she was going to let me sell her home but at the last minute she gave it to another agent, a man no less. I swear I really don't get people sometimes and why they lead you up the garden path.

I had to move on to the next one thinking about 'The Law of Attraction'. I just knew I had to do better. I had spoken to a recruitment person during the day, as I felt property management was where I needed to be and, strangely enough, if I had of stuck out my job in property management 12 months prior I would be moving into the townhouse I had bought off the plan the previous year. Never the less it was too late; you just can't go back. I had to move on from the 'what ifs'.

I thought at least if I got a job in property management it would give me a steady income and that's what I needed after all my wages were just a retainer so in other words once I got commission I would have to pay back John everything he had paid me. The weeks were dragging on not to mention adding up and I owed John up to that point well over $3500. I had to do something, otherwise I knew I may end up with nothing and I couldn't afford to get to that point.

I wanted this job to be great but it was not a busy office and there was another agent who was very popular in the area so it was very difficult to say the least. but I had to keep trying.

Every day I just wished my life would get better; meet someone nice and be financially independent, that's what I craved for. The last six years were terrible and God certainly wasn't listening to me anymore. I needed him to hear me and give me a break. As the days went on I found myself losing my faith. I was so stuck in this situation and I could not see the light at the end of the tunnel.

I was still looking for another rental and found a small house not far from where Bryce and I lived in our dream home. It was the right rental for me and I had to wait to see if I was approved. The property managers were so slow which is why I couldn't understand why they had a great position and I couldn't get one.

I appeared to be always waiting for something, which was a continual headache.

My eldest boy decided to get a tattoo even though he knew that I absolutely hated them. At first, he lied to me and said he didn't have it done but then whilst on facebook I came across the truth. It wasn't my place to tell him what to do at the age of nearly 22 but it was my business when I had bills piling up and gave me nothing towards living with me.

I was bewildered and realised there was something very wrong with this picture, what had I taught him? Why did he not have the need to be responsible? I was so disappointed and continued to blame myself for the way he was because I was the parent and I took my role seriously. Some would have said, kick him out. After all, he had caused me so much heartache over the years, however I knew who he was underneath. He was and is a wonderful, compassionate misunderstood person. He needs confidence and he does not realise his full potential. It was never meant to be this way I couldn't tell anyone how I felt, so lost and so lonely. No one to speak to, no one to help me turn my life around and I started to feel sick, really sick. I think it must have been stress but at that point, I didn't care. I had enough of life and I didn't believe I had enjoyed it at all.

Since I was 17 years of age, my life from that point always belonged to someone else. It was never about me and I sacrificed so much to give to all my children, although my two eldest would not agree with that. I had to keep in the top of mind 'whatever doesn't destroy us makes us stronger'.

I had to get over the way I was feeling and jump back on the listing trail in my job. I had to continue my pursuit of happiness and believe it would change for the better if I was to survive.

I remember one particular day was so much better than any other and I thought if only it could be like that every day I would never leave my job.

I had a buyer for a unit I had listed but I couldn't sign them up as there was no section 32 so I had to wait till the following Monday and hopefully they wouldn't change their minds. Then I had some other people interested in three other properties. I was so excited. I thought what if they all wanted to buy that would give me a great start in real estate and so much confidence. I felt things were starting to move and couldn't wait till the next week to get the sale.

In the meantime, I had a call from Melissa who was from a recruitment agency she said she would meet with me the following week. I had to cover all my bases but I didn't want to make any mistakes like I had previously, after all I knew if I had the choice I wanted to stay in my job and be successful. I had to stay positive and make it happen. I needed to believe in myself and have faith it would work out the way it was meant to. I needed to have purpose and financial independence.

My deal came together; I was so excited. My first sale – and I got both commissions as the lister and the salesperson which gave me 40% of the commission. It was a fantastic feeling!

Then there was the reality check. I wasn't going to see that money. There was only enough to pay back what John had already paid me as a retainer and I thought that was the part that was the hardest. It was the first job, and as I said, I really enjoyed it, but there wasn't nearly enough money and I wasn't a patient person when it came to money.

It was time to meet with the recruitment company and I had decided this time to exaggerate how long I had been in my current position. I had always been honest and it got me nowhere so I decided that if I wanted to get further I couldn't tell the truth this time. The position I had the interview for was 40 minutes driving time away from home, but the position as a senior property manager was one I wanted, as it was with a very reputable company that paid well. I got through the interview and they rang not long after to ask if I would meet with the CEO the next day. I was very nervous because when you tell one lie the rest of the lies follow but please remember I had to survive and it was my way or no way was I going to get the job. I had applied for over 100 jobs and no one cared how much trouble I went to, no acknowledgement at all. They call themselves recruitment company's, they say "we want you", in their advertisements but it's all just lies. They treat you like crap and don't care at all, not even just to send you a letter thanking you for sending your resume. I feel so sorry for anyone trying to get a position in today's world.

At the same time, I was served with a notice to quit which meant I had to leave the home I was renting within 60 days because relatives of the landlord's were moving in. I felt even though I wanted to move anyway and was just waiting on approval for another property to rent it was the universe's way of moving me on.

Then I received a letter from a debt collector which was a bit frightening and I had to wait till the next day to find out what that was about, obviously the restaurant and an account that was not paid.

It was all getting too much and I knew I really didn't want to leave my job. I knew patience was all that was required and a bit of front. I had a call from the recruitment company again to inform me that the CEO I had seen was very interested in me. I was shocked, it had been years I had been waiting for someone to say that, for a dream job paying what I wanted. I realised maybe I was not doing the right thing for me and went to my boss, John.

I asked him if he could make my retainer a little more and he agreed, so I stayed. He had so much faith in me and I decided that I would be far better off where I was after all the more money I got the more I was taxed and then there was travelling expenses, it wasn't worth it. John had given me a chance that no one else had to earn big money and all I had to do was get more confident which is what I planned to do. I was going to be a success and I wanted it so bad that is all I thought about. I had to work hard to attain that and I was prepared to do just that.

Chapter 17

KEEPING FAITH

Who remembers hearing, "Every day in every way I will get better and better", it is an old saying that I always loved and I would tell myself that every morning. Every time I dropped pamphlets in letterboxes for the business, I would say listings come easy to me repeatedly until they did. I wasn't about to let anything or anyone stand in my way.

My family was a mess and my work was all I had but more importantly I had come to realise I couldn't change the way my eldest children felt about me, that was just the way it was. My youngest boys were the only ones I knew I could depend on from time to time. The difference was between them and my eldest two they always got over our spats. We said what we had to say and then we would move on which is the way it should be.

The boys and I had realised that there was only the three of us and there was no one else to depend on, we were the family.

My mum was always there as well so it was time to put what was the family behind me and start over.

I had to concentrate on becoming a success and stop allowing thoughts of my family problems to disrupt my thinking. I had to stay focused and get rid of the disappointment I felt for my eldest children and their spouses to be a success.

I knew in my own mind once I moved house it would all fall into place. The real estate agent still had no answer for me and I was getting so frustrated by the continual wait. It was as if the place I had been living in was not letting me go. I had always believed it was full of bad karma because it was built on aboriginal ground and nothing good had happened there at all, in fact just the opposite. It had been the worst 16 months of my entire life, even worse than those bad relationships.

I continued packing I knew the coming week I should hear something after all it was another birthday and I was overdue for the next seven years of my life to begin. Isn't that what they say, every seven years your life changes? It all had to change; God knows it just had to. The cost of rental properties was ridiculously high. I couldn't comprehend how a normal family survived in today's world. What was ahead for my boys? Were they always going to live with me? How do young people move forward in today's world? My concern is probably the same as many parents around the world, because life wasn't what it used to be and always much more difficult being a single parent.

I was starting to feel confident and excited at the same time knowing that I was leaving the townhouse to a new place where happiness was waiting for me. I know many will say happiness in within but sometimes it is also about your surroundings.

I knew in my heart that my birthday was a new beginning and I would leave behind all the bad stuff. My youngest had an interview with a university on my birthday and I just knew it was going to be good. My other son was waiting to be accepted for his building course and I knew that would happen as well because he always was a practical person, not a studious one and was always meant to have a trade. My boys were the exact opposites and all I wanted for them was success and to be able to live a good life to survive in today's world comfortably.

Then and only then would I feel true happiness. I knew in my heart even though over those years I had so many issues of my own to deal with they knew that I had done a great job as a mother and I was sure they knew that to.

I still had no news from the property manager about the rental I so badly wanted and was getting rather anxious not knowing where I was going. My heart kept telling me to move closer to my daughter in Berwick although I knew that would be a disaster, as she had shown no concern for me as I was going through the restaurant fiasco. I knew my boys wanted to stay close to their friends and I just couldn't see harmony if I moved away although I believed it may have been best for them away from the alcohol and from some not so great friends who seemed to party all the time.

I was totally over the drinking and kids not taking responsibility for themselves at their age. When I think back to the way kids were years ago it really frustrated me so much. They just never seem to stand on their own two feet and constantly became a burden. They needed to become men.

It had been one of the loneliest weekends I had encountered and I really felt so isolated, no one cared and Christmas was coming. I had to get out of this state of mind I was in and packing was probably the best way to keep me occupied.

I needed to be ready just in case I was lucky enough to get the home I applied for and I wasn't sure what I was going to do if I missed out. I had to keep my faith that all would work out in the end.

My job with John was going slow and I had to remember it was Christmas so I needed to give it till February just to make sure it wasn't going to work for me although other people made it work so it should be the same for me I would tell myself continually.

I just couldn't accept that nothing was working in my life, why? I didn't understand what did I ever do to anyone and yet here I was facing all sorts of problems. I had to learn patience and discipline if I was to rise above it all. The two words I never understood.

I had received a rather disturbing letter from the man I had bought the restaurant from asking me for a few thousand dollars which was outrageous. It had been sent from his lawyer. I couldn't believe the gall of this man who had totally ripped me off. He maintained that I owed him for stock and wages which was absurd. I sent an email to his lawyer telling him to take me to court, as I owed nothing and believe me no man was going to rip me off again. I felt like I had been cursed with so much bad luck and couldn't understand why this was happening to me.

Was I playing the victim I would ask myself? Is that why all these nasty things were happening or was it the horrible unlucky home I lived in? Whatever the reason, it was totally unfair so I had to find a way of ignoring everything including both my sons' behaviour of late, every weekend they were partying. They seemed to be going back to their old ways and I had just about had enough. I never understood the way they thought when they saw what I was facing.

I started reading 'Follow Your Heart', by Andrew Matthews. Funnily enough it had been sitting next to my bed for months. It was the only book I had not packed or read. I think I must have bought it years prior and it just sat in my bookcase for some reason. I believe things happen for a reason and the same for books maybe there was a reason I was only reading it now.

The book was about believing in yourself and I realised I needed to stay optimistic no matter how bleak things may have looked. 'Follow Your Heart', was the reinforcement I was looking for and I knew I just had to believe that eventually everything would start to change for the better. Even though I said I was going to give my job with John till February another position had come up 50 minutes drive from home and I was lucky enough to get an interview. The opportunity was too good to miss. Financially it would help me get my own home over the next 12 months and that was the most important thing to me. I really needed that security.

I heard from the property manager finally for the home I applied for and I was the successful applicant so it was all happening. I felt I owed a lot to the book 'Follow Your Heart', I was reading because I was changing my thoughts however all the pressure was on me when I was told I could move into the property on Christmas Eve.

I knew this was going to be hard for me because there was only me. No one to help and I was alone. The boys helped me a little but then took off for the weekend again and out of control. I had to get the packing done but my depression got the better of me and I started drinking, the worst thing I could have done.

When one goes down this pathetic path it's because of the loneliness and no one to turn to. The next day I pulled myself together and continued reading this fabulous book, which somehow gave me the strength that I needed to get through the next week. Pack the house, get the position I applied for and move into my new home. It was all going to happen and from that point on I knew all would start to become normal again in my life after all it had been six years since there was any form of normality for me. I started feeling everything would be okay and then I thought when I am settled in the new rental maybe I would take up a hobby. I was thinking of golf with my eldest of the two boys because he was my biggest worry and he needed that closeness because Bryce was never going to be there for him.

I wanted and needed their lives to become normal because it had broken my heart over the years to see their lives in such turmoil and as I said the only real family they had was their nana and me.

Their sister was there occasionally and their eldest brother and his family had disowned us all even at Christmas including my poor mum. I had asked myself repeatedly why or how could this be?

They had disowned us the Christmas prior and only had come back when they wanted me to buy the restaurant, which is where all my troubles started. Families, as I said earlier, should be there for each other no matter what. I can't say that enough and I had always believed in unconditional love.

Everyone makes mistakes, even those closest to you and they had been so horrible with the restaurant fiasco but what could I do they just turned their backs on all of us. My eldest son and his wife had forgotten if it had not been for Bryce they would not have had their first home. We helped them so much in the past financially but, conveniently, they had forgotten that too.

I have to say Bryce was always good to my eldest son even more so than his own father. My daughter was the only one who was always self sufficient I never had a worry with her. As I said I maintain that love is unconditional and if you learn from your mistakes that is all that matters and everyone should be able to still move on and continue to be a family. No one should sit in judgment of others!

I had become bitter because of my situation and I knew I just had to concentrate on the boys and our new life. This was to be the week that everything changed for the better starting with getting this new position.

I got an email to say that the position would not become available for another month, which gave me time to give my sales job with John a chance and I wasn't sure at this stage whether I would even get a second interview so I decided if it was meant to be it would be.

I kept moving forward and we moved into a great house, which we all felt had good karma. I can't explain why it just felt good and the boys felt it too. Once I was unpacked it felt like home. I even unpacked boxes that had not been opened for years. Placed my family photos on the walls and just sat in awe as it felt so right.

Funny, I was reading my star sign and it said I was moving to a place that made me feel like I was coming home and that's exactly how I felt. I just wished every day I had the money to purchase the home although it was not for sale. I felt like we were meant to be here and it was just down the road from where my youngest boys went to kindergarten. It was also around the corner from where Bryce and I had built our first home.

So many memories, maybe too close to home, but still in many ways comforting.

Chapter 18

GOOD KARMA

Christmas was here, and it had to mean 2011 was going to be different from the previous year when the boys and I sat alone and had no one to share the festive season with. Everything was about to change. I just had that feeling.

My eldest sister had rung me the night before Christmas and asked the boys and me to celebrate the day with her family. I knew my youngest sister was going and she hadn't spoken to me for nearly 30 years so I was hesitant. I didn't want to put a damper on the day for everyone else. I had no idea why she hated me all those years. All I knew is that it started the day I left my first husband. No matter what we went through as kids, my sisters and I had a reasonably close relationship growing up but our family situation had affected us in different ways through Dad's drinking.

Even when our kids were little, we always looked after each other's children and we were all I thought quite close. My dad always had said to me that it was jealousy and even though our family was dysfunctional because of alcohol, we were still a close-knit family.

I had tried several times with her to make it right but she never wanted anything to do with me. Over the years, I just accepted the way it was. When my father died, I felt so resentful towards her as I felt she had robbed him of his family which I knew would have made him a very happy man had it all been resolved. It affects all of the family when one person creates such disharmony, at Christmas, birthdays and other special occasions. It is so wrong when families are so torn because of another's selfishness and ends up hurting everyone for no reason. On the other hand, I suppose we do not know what others are going through and she had many of her own problems. If families communicated, no one would ever be in these types of situations. As my mum always taught me, say what you think and get over it. It sounds so easy but I suppose it is not.

I decided to go after all to my sister's family Christmas. I thought, why should I be alone again? I needed and wanted them in my life. The boys and I always enjoyed their family. My sister had a beautiful family and they were so close even though her husband had passed away 7 years prior. He was a wonderful man and I think anyone that had known him still to this day misses him. He had died far too young and was the most amazing man, father and husband.

The day started off great; my eldest son of the two youngest brought me breakfast in bed which delighted me. He made me feel so special and we then had our own special morning together around the Christmas tree. Then it was off to my sister's festive

Christmas and we were all so happy to be there. She and her family had gone to so much trouble for everyone.

I walked in and my youngest sister was there; not a word was spoken between us. We had lunch and then gave out presents although I had nothing for anyone except my mum and that was okay because we had decided not to exchange gifts. My nephew who was playing Father Christmas handed me a present from my youngest sister. I didn't have my glasses on and could barely see who it was from so I asked my son to read it to me and I was shocked when he read it was from my youngest sister. I opened the present to find lovely gold earrings she had bought me. I can't tell you how I felt at that stage. It just blew me away and I had so many mixed emotions that brought tears to my eyes.

The war was finally over.

I waited until she was alone, walked up to her and asked the obvious question, why had she bought me a gift? Her reply was, "It's about time isn't it?"

With that, I said, 'I have nothing for you' and she said it didn't matter, so I kissed her and left it at that.

We didn't speak after that and I didn't want to push it. After all, it had been nearly 30 years and it had to repair slowly. I haven't heard from her since but I am sure that we are on the path to recovery. I just wish it had been when Dad was alive; I know Mum was so happy that she got to see it.

So you see, there is no reason to hold grudges in life, no matter what the reason.

When you are a family, it should go without saying. We should never sit in judgement of others; we may not agree with what others do, as that is their choice.

Who are we to say what is right and what is wrong? We all make our own life choices and we have to live with them but it should not affect or infect our lives with each other.

I feel I have grown so much these past six years since I asked Bryce to leave, even though they have been the worst years I have known.

Maybe that is why I am alone, to understand more about who I am? Although, I still don't understand why we have to go through so much pain when we are learning our lessons of life.

It had been the best Christmas Day that the boys and I had known for years. My family was getting back on track even though my eldest son had disowned us. He had his own lessons to learn but I felt it didn't matter anymore; after all, we all have the journey of life's lessons and his was no different. I could do nothing about it and had by this stage accepted his family's decision to disown us although it was sad for my grandchildren.

They were the ones that would suffer because of it. Two beautiful young girls who were 13 and 10 years old did not need this hostility in their lives. My son and his wife were not teaching them about love or forgiveness – all they were teaching them was anger and hatred.

One thing I know for sure, is that he will have so many regrets one day for the years he lost with his extended family and it was all for what?

It seemed I had gained a sister and lost a son? That didn't make any sense to me at all but it was what it was and there was nothing I could do to change the situation at all. I had texted my son twice before Christmas to put an end to it but got no reply so I had done all I could.

Life is a circle of change and sometimes it is out of our control so we just have to live with the choices that people make and accept them. I think that is what I have learned, the more you fight against the situation the worse it becomes, but when you accept where you are in life, it becomes easier to live with.

New Years Eve was upon us and there was no one at home. The boys had gone on separate road trips with their friends and I was alone again. I decided to take the time and reflect on the past and try to make sense of it. Ridiculous of course, but I started watching all the home videos that Bryce had made with his movie camera. I hadn't had the camera out of the box for years and I wanted to go down memory lane. It was funny and at the same time sad. It was a life I realised that was a happy one at times. There was no doubt in my mind watching the boys with their dad in the videos that there were some really happy times and I knew no one could take those memories from me.

What I learned whilst watching them was that even though Bryce was so unfaithful so many times, I had to question myself? What part did I play in the demise of our marriage? I knew that his infidelity was not because of anything I had done. He had always been that way even before I had met him but I should not have looked at that as an excuse for drinking too much. It never helped anything it just made it all so much worse.

I am not excusing his behaviour, which I think led to my drinking but, at some point, you have to question the part one plays in the demise of a relationship?

It made me realise that if we both had tried and he could have focused on his family, we would have had a great life as a family. The boys would have been so different. They would have been more confident and secure in their lives, which would have made a huge difference to them both. My eldest of the two would not have so much anger in him and they both would have had stable lives.

My reflection was well worth it because it showed me that we were still a family whether Bryce was with us or not. I sent him a text on New Year's Eve saying to him that I had been watching our home videos and he was a great dad when the boys were small and my wish for him was that he could have a close relationship with his sons again if he wanted. It did not have to be this way. They were not close at all and even though he had remarried, it should not make any difference.

Dads are so important through their son's eyes. They look at their dad as their role model. Boys watch and listen to everything that daddy says and does. That becomes the end product, a chip off the old block, so maybe now I should be saying just as well they didn't have that at all.

I probably shouldn't say that, because Bryce could have taught his sons things that would have made a huge difference to them.

I wanted that so much for our boys, as they had been cheated by not having their dad in their lives and Bryce was living in Queensland so far away. I do not know how, but hopefully one day they will mend and be together again.

It is hard to undo the past but we can change the future at any time, just a word or gesture makes all the difference.

Every child needs the love of their parents no matter how old they are. We all suffer and carry with us the rejection we feel through our journey in life.

New Year's Eve was hard but I now am so grateful that I am where I am and it will only get better from here. I know that and feel that giving is the answer for all of us in life. It is not what we get in life; it is about what we give. It is not about what happens to us, it is how we deal with it.

There are always less fortunate people in the world who have real problems in life but it does not make our own lives any less painful by realising that either. Maybe awareness is the word I am looking for because when we are aware of what is going on around us in the world we become more grateful

Chapter19

THE YEAR AHEAD

Optimism is what I needed to focus on and I relied on my wonderful books to help me keep on track. There was no way I was going to allow myself to be stuck in life's vicious circle again. It was full steam ahead from this point and I was ready for the year ahead.

I sent my youngest sister a Happy New Year message. I thought it would be small steps to get us back on track and she replied with a good response, I knew this was the beginning to getting our family back together. I felt at this stage there was nothing I could not achieve. My family was the most important to me and I knew going back to the beginning was right, establishing the relationships that were lost somewhere in the last 30 years.

Watching the home videos on New Year's Eve made me homesick for Bryce. He was a great dad when the boys were so little and I knew he could be again. If he only just realised what he was missing. I only wished we could have made it work and he had not have been so unfaithful to all of us. I just felt we were great at times together but there was no point looking back; he was married now and life would never be the same anyway. Once the trust is gone, there is no way you can repair a relationship. I knew that because of when I took Bryce back in 1992. I was kidding myself. I thought I could rebuild that trust but realistically you never can. Once the circle of trust is broken, you can never go back. In saying that, I have to remember there are those that I have known that have mended their relationships. However, if they were truly honest, I am sure they will never forget the betrayal and every now and again they find themselves mistrusting all over again.

It is something that never truly leaves you.

I think I realised I had been mourning the past six years. It's like when someone dies you can't get them back and it doesn't matter what we think and how much we wanted it to turn out so differently, what's done is done.

I often wonder if he thinks of us, whether he misses us as a family or even cares. It would be nice to know. I truly loved him back then and he will never know how his actions hurt all of us, particularly our sons. It breaks my heart to think I was never enough and realistically, as I said, the grass is never greener on the other side. Eventually he will have karma as I did, so will Brad.

No one goes without learning eventually that life's mistakes come back to us. I often wondered if Bryce had regrets, maybe or maybe not. Was he a callous shallow person? Who knows? Those are the unanswered questions I will take to my grave. But I loved him and I will probably never love anyone else that way again. After all, we were together 22 years. You hear so often about men leaving their wives after they have been married 25 years and I will never understand that. They should be best friends and how could someone leave their best friend for someone they hardly know, unless of course they had good reason. Most of the time though it is just because of lust.

He missed out on so much whether he knows it or not. His children in their teens, the family and the wonderful moments I was so privileged to have. He missed it all and even though there have been so many problems with the boys, there have also been wonderful times too.

No one can get those moments back. I wonder if he ever thinks about the time he missed his youngest son's first steps and his first birthday party, all those years ago, in 1992 when he left us the very first time. He missed celebrating all their birthdays and every Christmas the last six years and I cannot for the life of me, comprehend how any man can just put their children to one side and not give them another thought. It is beyond comprehension!

I would not trade it for the world to miss those magical moments, warts and all.

My younger boys had over the years shown me such love even though they had given me grief and of late, they have gone back to their bad habits. I don't know why they are continually in this party frame of mind with no responsibility. I think it is the new generation.

I don't know how to change anything right now so I just ride the storm as usual. I have come to believe the more I fight with them about their behaviour the worse it gets; so it is best left alone, even though they should have part-time or at least casual jobs at their age whilst they are studying.

As a parent, I know I am not the only one who has this problem; they just seem to lack responsibility for themselves after all they are in their 20's.

I emailed Bryce this morning just to ask his advice; I wanted him to understand that our boys were heading on this path of destruction and I needed his help. I didn't expect him to come to the rescue but he was still their dad and he hadn't seen his youngest for so long who was at this stage becoming the worst of the two with alcohol. I realised alcoholism ran in our genes but it wasn't just that it was the way young ones were today, it's a different world.

Bryce replied to my email and for the first time acknowledged my situation. He said I should get a one-bedroom unit and then the boys would have no choice but to live on their own.

Quite true, but so unrealistic! I could never see my sons on the street and I realise it may be easy for some to do that but not for me. I am a mother and they are my children even if they were adults. I needed to find another way to bring them to their senses.

I had been watching the series 'Brothers and Sisters', the boys had given me the box set for Christmas and it made me realise I did not have a crazy family. The mother in the series was no different to me but my family was. The family in the series argued a lot but got over their arguments and still loved each other. This was the way my mother had raised me, but in my family they just didn't get over their arguments. They hung on to every word that was said, at least that was the eldest two from my first marriage, who both continued to make my family dysfunctional.

I realised that my eldest son and daughter had so much jealousy all these years for the youngest two, that our family was never going to be like the Walkers on the series, which was really sad.

It should not make a difference how many children are in a family, how many fathers there are, or how much age difference there is between them. They all still should love each other and be there for each other. That was my impression of my perfect family and I blamed my eldest two for making it the way it was.

I knew that my family would never change. It had been like this since the boys were born and there was nothing I could do about it. The eldest two always picked on my mistakes and believed I loved the youngest two more which was not true however I had come to resent the eldest two for not allowing our family to be just that 'a family'.

It was Sunday morning and I woke to find my youngest had not come home. I had come to the stage of always saying to myself no news is good news but it wasn't easy. At least if they had their own place, I would get used to that and I would stop worrying whether they were okay.

I awoke so depressed thinking about the lost girl on her 17th birthday finding out she was pregnant all those years ago and the sacrifices she had made. It was like thinking of someone else rather than realising it was me.

I had a choice even back then; I didn't have to go through with having a child but I did. I was such a naïve girl and we were not educated about sex like the kids are today. My eldest children's father was my first sexual experience. He was as naïve as me and as they say the rest is history.

I awoke feeling cheated out of a life; after all, I didn't know what it was like to be a teenager or fulfil my dreams to be an actress or even a lawyer. They were the two professions I had wished for when growing up, ever since I can remember. I realised had I had my head screwed on properly, I could have gone back to school after I had my first baby, but I didn't. What I am saying, is that life is a choice and no matter what happens to us we do have a choice if we stay focused on our own lives. I didn't have to give up my dreams I could have still pursued them and life would have been so different for me. It was always about someone else, looking after everyone except my needs and me. I think that is what most mothers do without realising and then it is too late.

I am at the point now where I need to think of my life and just me in it because all my children even though I still have two at home they had their own lives and I was on the outer.

I needed to focus on where I was going and accept that I was alone.

I knew that my eldest two were very close and my eldest son and daughter-in-law were the cause of my isolation from family. My daughter was very close to them and it was obvious she had no loyalty to me. She believed nothing I said. My daughter-in-law had poisoned her mind against me. There was nothing I could do, or wanted to do by this time, I just had to accept they were all out of my life.

As a mother, I did the best I could and there was no way I could fix anything without being accused of having an ulterior motive. I was and am a big believer in loyalty to one's family; it wasn't that I wanted anyone to take sides I just wanted them to believe my side of the story with the restaurant fiasco, but no one ever did. I couldn't understand why my own daughter would believe my daughter-in-law over me. Everything that came out of her mouth was a lie. She was the one who made my life a living hell when we were in the restaurant and destroyed my family along with my eldest son. I do believe in karma and I know one day the truth will come out. It was strange to think of my daughter-in-law that way because I thought we were close at one time but I suppose you never really know anyone.

I had not heard from the companies with whom I had second interviews and I hoped that would be soon. In the meantime, it had given me enough time to appreciate where I was with John, selling real estate.

I had never stayed long enough to see if I could make it in previous positions and I had time on my side to make the right decision where I was meant to be. I really enjoyed working for John and his personal assistant. They had become like family even though we were all so totally different. When I think about it, I believe it was because we didn't judge each other and criticize each other for anything.

I had listed and sold one property in the last two months but, keeping in mind it was the Christmas period, it wasn't a clear indication of what could be. With the book 'The Secret', sitting next to my bed, I just knew it may be worth hanging on for a while. I really believed in the power of the mind. I knew now was the time to put what 'The Secret' had been telling me to the test and becoming patient was a big part of that.

I needed to build relationships in the community, stay focused, work hard and believe success was not too far away.

I wondered how I had come to where I was living and working and had realised three years prior I had looked at the home I was living in to buy at the same time I had dropped my résumé into the real estate office I was working at.

At that time, I could have bought the home I am now living in but thought the back yard was too small. I never heard from the real estate agent back then about my résumé, but here I was in the now and for some unexplainable reason, I was where I was meant to be. John had bought the real estate office three years after I had submitted my résumé. It all had to mean something. Life is full of unknown messages and if I didn't believe it then, I certainly do now. Instincts also play a very big part in one's life and where you end up. Successful people use their instincts.

My life had not been kind to me for many reasons even though I had made so many sacrifices and writing this book has enabled me to keep my sanity.

Writing about everything that had happened to me was so confronting and I was able to understand it so much more clearly. It has been an amazing journey for me to be able to take a closer look at myself because there is so much to understand about why we are so driven by emotions.

I became preoccupied and worried about one of my sons who had started seeing a woman with two children, 12 years his senior, and I was so worried about history repeating itself but there was nothing I could do.

I remember when Bryce and I started dating; no one could have told me I was so in love. I had to let go and let him make his own mistakes whether I agreed or not. I had no control over that situation.

He was such an angry young man and I suppose if I were to be honest, he was the worry of my life but there was no way I was going to interfere. I suppose now I appreciate how Bryce's mum and dad must have felt when his son of 20 was going out with a woman of 28 with two children. They must have been horrified.

I could never understand why they were so upset, but I do now.

That's what happens to all of us on our life journey. We understand very little when we are younger but, as you age, you do have a better understanding of how parents felt when we thought we knew it all and then it happens to us. We become the parents. All of a sudden, we are learning.

Fortunately, the relationship between my son and the older woman fizzled out and I felt relieved to say the least.

It is sad really, because we never get how someone else feels until it happens to us. I suppose that is how life is and for my sons I wanted normality, which is probably what Bryce's parents wanted for him. It would be nice to be able to tell them that I understand now but it is too late. They have both passed on. Yet another lesson for me!

That's what life teaches us; never wait to say the things you want to say to anyone particularly those you love otherwise it's too late when they are gone.

Life is about lessons as we get older and some things are just too hard to learn but we have to learn them whether we like it or not. I am told that our lessons in life keep repeating themselves until we understand what they are meant to teach us. I now get it!

I needed to let my younger boys go and let them find their own lives. I had no control any longer. I just hoped it would turn out right for all of us. We were in a good place, the home we lived in did have good karma and it was a nice feeling.

I had a lot riding for the following week to see if I could make it in real estate and this time I had a good feeling about it.

Chapter 20

DREAMS BECOME REALITY

My week went well. I now had four listings on the board and I was so excited. I started to see the bigger picture and knew I was where I was meant to be. It was all falling into place. It's true what they say with everything we do, you have to put in the hard yards to see results.

My eldest of the two boys, or should I say men, by this time was starting his pre-apprentice course in building and my youngest was accepted into university to become a PE teacher, secondary and primary. I was over the moon and I have to say that is when any mother or father who has done it on their own can say it was all worth it. Maybe now the boys would settle down and they will now have the opportunity for their lives to come together and put all the anger behind them.

As I said, I knew they loved me and I knew eventually they would find their lives, have great careers and perhaps grow a wonderful family themselves. I knew without a doubt that they would make great dads because they knew looking at their own father that they could never put anyone through what they had to endure.

I realised at this point that this was going to be the hardest challenge of my life. My eldest children had deserted me and I didn't know whether they would ever come back into my life.

I knew that financially it was now or never, I had to make it work. I was grateful my youngest boys were starting a new chapter in their lives, as we all had to move on.

I thought, maybe now some normality for them but I was still the one who had to deliver financially and that had been a struggle in itself.

I had picked up another two listings and I knew that wasn't enough, so every day I would drop pamphlets and make calls. I needed now to make some sales. I knew in myself that it was now all achievable but it would not happen overnight and the end result was up to me. There was no one else if it was going to be it was up to me.

I was working six days a week and feeling exhausted but I had to keep going. It's an awful feeling when there is no one to share all the burdens with. I think so many couples take for granted what they have because when you are on your own it's just you and only you that have to be the responsible one for everyone and everything.

Finally I made another sale although there was not much commission in it for me because it was another office's referral but never the less it was a sale. I felt I was moving forward but very slowly at least the signs were there. I was not about to give up I knew it was only a matter of time before I would get on my feet. It was hard to stay positive knowing my eldest son and daughter wanted nothing to do with me. I felt myself on occasion slipping into a depression but somehow always managed to pull myself up.

Every time I felt myself feeling that way I told myself that it was just emotions and as I said so many times it is not what happens to you it's how you deal with it. This was the way I had conditioned myself to deal with my thoughts.

I knew I had to say, 'stop', every time I felt myself going under and it seemed to be working. I was starting to focus on my job and by this time I really loved where I was working.

It's funny how certain people come into our lives to give us more information than we bargained for.

One of our landlords came in and the irony of it was that Bryce had worked with her many years prior. She had recognised me from when I was on Council and knew that I was Bryce's ex-wife.

 She spoke about Bryce and how she knew him, which was not flattering at all to him. He was worse than I had thought which took me back to a place I didn't want to remember. The memories were hard enough but to know he was such a womaniser was so degrading to me and as she said such a manipulator.

It's true that sometimes the people that work with your partner in life know so much more about your life than you do! I shrugged it off and knew I was not going to let it get under my skin although it did at first. Once again, I thought I had come to terms with the man I had known for 22 years but in actual fact I didn't know him at all. It just seemed so surreal.

I had a call from another potential client and this time it was an up market property in the marina. I was so excited. Another listing I wanted so badly.

The vendor had several agents giving appraisals and I just kept saying to myself that I would be the winner in the end. Keeping a positive mind is one of the most powerful tools you can have. It paid off; the vendor rang just before I was about to leave the office one afternoon and he told me I was the most professional. He gave me the listing. The property was absolutely beautiful and worth about 1.2 million dollars. I was over the moon. My listings were growing and I knew the sales would come.

This was a pivotal moment in my working life. I had come to realise the two major lessons I had not learned were here to teach me, discipline and patience. I had never stayed anywhere long enough the last six years to give anything time to work and maybe I had never really worked hard enough. I expected it would all just come to me and if it didn't happen quickly then I had the mindset that it wasn't going to happen. I never thought of myself as lazy but maybe more because of the lack of confidence that had been stripped away from me piece by piece over the years.

If I didn't have confidence in a sales role how could anyone else believe in me?

I had never had a problem with confidence in my professional life before I went into Council as an elected member. I think from that moment when I left the newspaper along with everything that happened with Bryce my life started to crumble around me. It was the beginning of losing all my self-confidence personally and professionally.

I felt the happiest I had felt for some time that day, realising my professional life was moving forward. I had to focus on getting to the top of my career and not allow my personal issues to get in the way.

I was starting to believe in who I was and looked forward to pursuing my goals. I cared about people I wasn't just another real estate sales person. I felt I was better than that. I treated people the way I liked to be treated. I believed in honesty and always doing what was right for my vendors. I didn't cut corners or look at people like some agents did as just another client.

In the meantime, I had a crisis at home. My eldest of the two boys was not doing well. I didn't realise for some time that he had gone back to his old ways, drinking too much alcohol. I couldn't understand why he would go back to this way of life when his life was finally coming together. He had thrown one of his tantrums and started lashing out which is when I realised I had a real problem. I had to try to get through to him and I didn't know how because alcohol affects every person differently. He was one of those people who get so angry and the language was what no mother should have to endure. I thought we were all on the same page and everyone was getting their lives on track. I was hurt and angry at the same time but I had to find a way to help him.

I really couldn't understand his behaviour as he was nearly 22 years of age and he had put my youngest and I through so much. I had moments where I was reliving my childhood and I didn't deserve that.

Alcoholism is bad enough and mixed with other substances is so much worse. He should have been happy he didn't realise that going down this path was not going to allow him to see happiness or success.

How I was going to help him? I didn't know and felt he was on a path of destruction. At this point, I had to think of my youngest. I had hardened up a little and he wasn't going to stay with me if he couldn't change. He needed to see a doctor and work out what was going on but he wouldn't and if I pushed it he would lash out at me. I had become frightened by this stage because his temper was the worst I had ever lived with and I found myself becoming frightened like a child.

I deserved better.

I had done everything for my children; except they weren't children anymore and yet here I was still looking after them at the age of 20 and nearly 22. I knew there was something wrong with that picture; after all, my eldest two were out of home by the time they were 18. There is a lot to be said about the different generations and that is what they were.

They didn't even pay board; they didn't get it at all. Maybe it was my fault because I had always done so much for them. They never went without. They didn't know what it was to work hard either although my youngest at least had casuals jobs on the odd occasion.

I thought I was doing all the right things as a parent but maybe I was making my own situation worse. I had to look at the part I had played in all of it. As the old saying goes you have to be cruel to be kind but I could never be that cruel person which was my downfall.

I looked to Bryce for help but he was not interested at all so I had no choice but to deal with it.

Chapter 21

GETTING BACK ON TRACK

I felt so overwhelmed by this stage and yet I knew I had to stay focused. I couldn't allow the issues with my son to take me back to the space I had been. I knew he could change if I could find a way to get through to him. I had decided I would give him an ultimatum either he got off the substances he was taking or he would have to move out.

I was fearful of doing that because I knew I could make the situation so much worse but that to me was making him responsible for his own life and his own choices. I had always believed in taking responsibility for the choices one makes in life and this was no different. There is accountability for everyone and at this stage, he had to know that.

I couldn't keep helping him and covering up his mistakes. I wasn't going to put up with anymore abuse in my life it just had to be over.

It only takes one person to upset a family and I had so many disappointments with most of my children surely I had the power to make it change. So much for the perfect family I had always dreamt of ever since I was a child. I didn't know by this stage whether it would ever happen and if everyone would ever live a normal happy life. I felt like a failure but I knew I had done the best I could at the time.

I started thinking of the past, which I did so often trying to make sense of my life. I had realised had I stayed married the first time I would have been married 39 years. I will never forget being that naive girl of just 17 years of age, giving up my life to become a mother. Now looking back, I don't know where all the years went to and yet still no life of my own. I could never have a normal relationship with anyone again even if I wanted to as long as I was living in a situation filled with problems.

I really didn't care by that stage, although my closest friend lived in Brisbane she had been on her own for 16 years. She had the occasional relationship but nothing really serious until now. She had given up on anyone coming into her life and wasn't looking to be with another man.

She had a great job and her own home she didn't need anyone in her life but then life presented her with a guy who she has now been with for some time. She had met him years prior but for some reason had never taken an interest; maybe the time wasn't right back then. She had two boys of her own and gone through her own heartache but once she had dealt with all of that and had total independence life changed. I thought maybe there was hope for me yet.

I couldn't think about meeting anyone. I had to get my son back on track and focus on my job. Nothing was going to hold me back and I wasn't about to lose my son to a society of mixed up kids.

He had to change. I had to have faith. There was no one to help me and I knew somehow I had to get him to have more confidence in himself. We had gone down this path so many times, the ups and the downs. I wasn't about to give up I had to somehow find the answer to yet another nightmare.

I knew the person he was when he wasn't out of control. He was the kindest hearted human being anyone could ever meet. He had always been so health conscious and could have done anything that he set his mind to. When anyone takes any type of substance whether alcohol or anything else it changes them completely and they don't realise what is happening to them or what they put anyone else through.

Why I have to go down this path over and over is unreal to me. I had been through enough in my life and I was going through so many emotions but I couldn't let it get the better of me.

He promised me that he would stop behaving this way and start concentrating on making his life better. His building class had been cancelled for two weeks and a friend had got him a trial with his boss to become an apprentice plumber for a few days. I couldn't understand I felt he was grasping at straws but never the less it would keep him focused for a few days and maybe then he would realise what he really wanted.

My son's best friend Dave was always there for both the boys when they needed someone to lean on. He had known them since primary school and had been through his own problems because of divorce but had managed to carve out his career earlier than most and both the boys respected him for what he had achieved. He was like a brother to them both.

It seems there are many young people in this generation that think that life owes them something and it is just one big party. They are not like the generations before us when we had to take on responsibility at such a young age. When I think about Bryce and even though he was on his own from 17 years of age he certainly didn't turn out to be any different. He took no responsibility at all for anyone but himself. I suppose I sound angry and I am!

Sometimes I think my life could have been so different had it not been for Bryce coming into my life. Maybe I would have been much happier had I not met him but then on the other hand I have my sons. That is a blessing in itself for many reasons. Maybe that is what it was all about.

Even though my life has been far from normal, I am grateful I have them in my life as I said warts and all. At least they know the meaning of family.

I had sold another two properties and I was so excited because I was nearly at the point where I had paid my retainer back and I could start seeing some commission. John was going away for a week, which gave me an opportunity to make some in-roads whilst he was gone. I wanted to list and sell more than I had before. I was the best at what I did and I was starting to believe it.

Much to my surprise, work was becoming my saviour. It was my turn and I was about to embark on a new journey one that would see me financially independent which was what I had always hoped for.

I have learned so much these past six years, actually nearly seven now. It has been the hardest road travelled for me but the knowledge I have now will give me the success I have yearned for.

I had learned that it was all about hard work, patience and discipline that can take you to wherever you want to be in life. I had learned that looking back creates so much negativity and that alone had stopped me from moving forward but I was in a good space now I just had to keep focused on my goal. When I talk about financial independence, it is not all about money. It was about success and regaining my self-esteem that had been stripped away from me since I was 17 years of age.

My eldest sister had called me and invited me away with her family. It wasn't for another month and I needed the money so I could get away. It would only be for a few days but it was important to me to have some time to relax and it had been so many years since we had all spent quality time together.

Chapter 22

EMPOWERING MYSELF

I had finished my boring Sunday reading 'The Law of Attraction'. I felt it was always good to fill my head with positive thoughts before I went to sleep. I had read this book before some years prior and thought it was time to reinforce what I already knew.

The next morning I arrived at work earlier than usual and John was away. He entrusted the office to me for the week. It didn't start off too well as one of our vendors had decided not to accept one of my contracts for the purchase of his property but my attitude was to stay positive and believe someone else would come along.

I did however list a property in the afternoon. John and I had presented to the vendor together to get the listing, and I had been left to do the work, so I was at least hoping he would share the commission with me.

I had decided that this was the week that was going to see me with a sale and that is what I would focus on. Nothing was going to interfere with my thoughts. I even started meditating every morning, giving me a clear head before I started work. I had never mastered meditation.

I don't know why it was just that I couldn't turn off my thoughts and the many self help books I had read all said meditation was a great way to start and finish the day.

I know everything takes time but it is always hard when you are waiting for your life to change. It was patience I was lacking; I found it hard to wait for anything. All the success that one is supposed to experience in life takes so long to happen.

I often thought to myself was it just me who felt like that or is everyone the same after all I had done everything 'The Secret', had told me.

I had read the book and watched the video twice but still I couldn't see myself making inroads and realised maybe that was the problem. I had to retrain the way I thought to start to see positive outcomes. I had to see and feel the end result of where I wanted to be. It's all about thoughts matching your feelings they must be the same. You have to feel as if it has already happened.

That excitement, that feeling of such confidence makes all the difference in the world. Just imagine if you had no doubts in yourself and you just sailed through life, it would be like winning tatts lotto. I think what I am trying to say is having faith in yourself is the beginning of success.

I was starting to tune in to my positive side and I knew it was only a matter of time before I would feel that type of power. I knew it was all about time and continual persistence. I always kept top of my mind the law of attraction and what it would bring. As I said the vendor did not accept the contract but that same morning a man appeared in the office who I had not seen before.

He asked me about some properties I had on the waterfront and I gave him the one that I hadn't sold because of the vendor not accepting the former offer. I stayed positive and that same afternoon a woman, who was the gentleman's wife who had come in earlier, appeared in the office. She asked me to show her through the property. They were not interested in the home only the land as they were looking to build their dream home. As soon as she saw it, she put an offer, $100,000 more than the previous offer I had presented to the vendor.

I was over the moon and thinking the law of attraction does work; however, I had to wait another three days to see whether the sale would go through.

I decided I would use the law of attraction every time I thought of my two boys particularly the eldest.

He appeared to be so stressed starting his building course and he had become very hard to live with. I needed to stop and think differently towards him. I needed to stop focusing on his behaviour and start to see him in a different light.

No matter what happened and what mood he was in, I kept my focus on his career, seeing him as a great builder. This was going to take time but in my mind I knew one day my thoughts would become reality. I kept telling him how well he was doing and in turn I knew that he would start believing in himself.

I think as parents maybe we lose sight of the bigger picture and that actually is what is missing in every aspect of our lives.

We don't believe in ourselves enough or those around us. It's funny when you start to change the way you think everything starts to change around you and you start to see things as they should be.

The offer on the property I was hoping for didn't go through and I was not about to give up. I had come too far and I knew I had to stay focused. I needed to concentrate on my negotiating skills to get this deal through.

The purchasers at first were hesitant to make another offer but I just stayed focused I knew in the end I would win. Every night for a week I would wake up in the morning and go to bed at night visualising the sold sign on the property. It was going to happen! The purchasers raised their price twice but still the vendor wanted more and by this time I was becoming frustrated. The property I felt was not worth more than what had been offered we were up to $1,145,000 it wasn't enough.

It was coming down to the wire; the vendor had changed his mind and dropped the price to $1,175,000. Was this ever going to end? Negotiations had gone on for a week; I wanted this sale to come to fruition and at the same time, although exhausting, it was a great learning curve for me.

Remember I said I was always impatient? I could never wait for anything personally or professionally which was my problem, but this experience was what I needed to be successful.

I had always been of the belief that everything happens for a reason and that had become so clear after this experience.

Whilst I was waiting for this deal to come to an end I picked up another two listings. Everything was moving and I felt so excited!

It was all going to happen for me the life I finally deserved.

Every now and again I would fantasise about the perfect man I would like in my life but, as I said to Kristee, my dear friend, whom I worked with, I had come to the stage in my life if I couldn't have the best I would rather have nothing. Financial independence had become so important to me after so many losses. I knew that the universe was teaching me the patience and discipline I needed to make my dreams come true.

My daughter finally had come back in my life although after looking at her facebook site, I felt a sense of betrayal.

She had gone away on holidays with her father, stepmother, close friends and my eldest son's family. They were having a wonderful holiday and didn't care at all about me or what their younger brothers were going through. We weren't welcome at all; none of them wanted us there. I wanted my family so badly to be a family but I could not compromise my principles. My eldest son and daughter even though they were my children, did not take after me. They were more their father's children and frankly they had proven to me that I was not that important to them anymore.

Whether there are two children in a family or six, every child is born with their own personality and even though they are brought up in the same family, their principles and values can be all so different.

By this time, I was completely over it and my daughter was so oblivious to what was right and wrong where family was concerned. She did not understand what loyalty meant; or maybe she did, but her loyalty was not to me. I could not understand how she could put her sister-in law before me. This woman was married to my eldest son; and had caused so many problems in my family since I had bought the restaurant. She had no conscience at all.

I knew at this point I couldn't try and salvage anything. My family was never going to be perfect or anywhere close to it. My daughter and her brother were people I really didn't know. I loved all my children unconditionally I just didn't understand why they were so hurtful. Family was everything to me and I had tried to give all my children everything they needed but I had come to realise that there obviously was something that maybe I didn't get right.

My younger boys had always been so different and as inconsiderate as they could be sometimes they still had compassion for others. I knew that they were no different to me as far as their principles and values were concerned.

I decided I was not going to allow my thoughts to stray. I had to keep focused on my life and reject all the negative thoughts I would have from time to time. I had to stay on track if I was going to make it on my own.

I believed so much by this time in The Law of Attraction and I was so focused on my future.

I could not force my eldest children to be closer to me and I had made up my mind just to accept the way they felt about me and move on with my life.

The only thing that I needed to focus on was closing my deal and getting on with it, nothing else was important to me at that time.

I was a tough negotiator and I knew this deal was going to happen. Life had been exhausting and lonely to say the least since Bryce and I divorced but I have to say I have learned so many valuable lessons for which I am grateful. Even though I am still by myself my experiences in life have taught me that whatever life throws at me I know I will cope.

I was so proud of my eldest of my younger boys he was really getting his life together. He had given up all his addictions and was completely focused on his building career. Life was changing again and I was starting to see my younger boys getting their lives together. That is all I ever wanted for them to realise they could be whoever they wanted to be. Clearly they were, out of all my children, the ones who had the principles of life that were so important to me and I was grateful for that because they had gone through so much over the past six years. They deserved to be happy.

My eldest of the two had met a lovely young woman named Beth who I am hoping will be by his side for a long time. I believe she was his inspiration. Isn't that how the old saying goes there is always a good woman behind every successful man?

The coming week was going to be interesting as I hoped to sell at least three properties and list a couple more. I was starting to see glimpses of what I could achieve. Life was starting to be wonderful again and I knew if I continued to monitor my thoughts and feelings I would make it all happen. I truly believe that is the secret to success.

As The Law of Attraction tells us, every time you have a negative thought change it to a positive and everything will be as it should be. It truly does work and I think that is what makes the difference between success and failure. Just imagine if there were no bad thoughts we would all be very successful and life would be a much happier place. I only wish it had not taken me all these years to understand the importance of monitoring thoughts and how easy it is to change the way we think and feel.

Visualisation also plays an important part of making dreams a reality. I wanted so badly to sell a property close to my heart for the vendors so I wrote sold across the flyer I had on my desk and imagined it sold. A few days later it did sell, it was truly amazing.

My big sale finally went through and then for the next month I listed another 12 homes and sold eight. My goal was to be the best and that was exactly where I was heading, I had no doubt.

Now looking back, I could see where I had been. The emotions I had experienced through bad relationships. The decisions I had made whilst going through emotional turmoil, ending in disaster. I finally for the first time was starting to experience my own life and that was what all the lessons were about as painful as they were.

I am so confident now in whom I am and I now know the world is my oyster. I hope that one day I will find the relationship I so richly deserve and have waited all my life for but I am in no hurry.

Life can be great and none of what I went through was really necessary had I listened to my instincts and learned to control my emotions. That is the key to keeping your sanity. I have learned so much about the pattern of our thoughts and how powerful our mind really is. I have let go of my anger, rejection, hate, fear and feelings of betrayal.

We can be whoever we want to be no matter what our background. I have come to love my life now and I know I will have continued success no matter what lies ahead.

I now know discipline and patience.

I have four wonderful children and I am proud of them all no matter what has happened between us. My eldest son, Jack, even though he has hurt me so deeply has no idea of what I think of him, which I find sad. I am and have always been proud of him.

He does a very difficult job as a psychiatric nurse and I do admire him for that every day of my life.

My successful daughter, Summer, who is so special to me, I will cherish forever. She is not only beautiful but has her own successful business and an amazing life. I know she will always find her way.

My two youngest sons are finally on their way to successful lives. I waited so long but I know now it will happen and even though they had an absentee father, they have learned so many valuable lessons. When or if they have children they will understand more than most the value of being a great dad and I know for sure they will be the best dad a child could have.

My youngest son, Luke, is on his way to becoming a teacher and my eldest son, Craig, a great builder.

I am so proud of their achievements and grateful for everyday they are part of my life.

They truly know and understand the true meaning of family.

I will leave you with something always to remember.

Life was never meant to be easy, and all families face the controversy with each other but please always remember, have your say and get over it because nothing is worth giving up family for.

Success is not just about your work it is also about your family.

I call it unconditional love.

Family is a circle of strength and love

THE END

Printed in Australia
AUOC010845171111
250840AU00002B/1/P